Cold Cash for Warm Hearts

101 Best Social Marketing Initiatives

Other titles co-authored by Dr. Richard Steckel:

Making Money While Making a Difference: How to Profit with a Nonprofit Partner

Filthy Rich: How to Turn Your Nonprofit Fantasies into Cold, Hard Cash

In Search of America's Best Nonprofits

Cold Cash for Warm Hearts

101 Best Social Marketing Initiatives

Dr. Richard Steckel
Elizabeth Ford, Casey Hilliard and Traci Sanders

High Tide Press
2004

Published by High Tide Press, Inc.
3650 West 183rd Street, Homewood, Illinois 60430

Copyright © 2004 Richard Steckel

All rights reserved under International and
Pan-American Copyright Conventions

Steckel, Richard, Cold cash for warm hearts: 101 best social
marketing initiatives /
by Richard Steckel, Elizabeth Ford, Casey Hilliard
and Traci Sanders –1st Ed.

ISBN 1-892696-32-0

Book and cover design by Frank Alatorre

Printed in the United States of America

First Edition

To Shelli, who makes getting up each morning worthwhile and exciting
–RS

To Richard for giving me a chance, my husband Dan for cheering me on, and the handful of mentors in my life who inspire me to work with purpose and passion.
–EF

To Jeff, Maddie, and Josh, the best inspirations any writer could ask for.
–TS

Table of Contents

Foreword 1

Introduction 3

Seniors
    Interaction 5
    Comfort 7
    Public garden 9
    Volunteerism 11
    Retirement planning 12

Children
    Outdoor adventure 15
    Advocacy 19
    Business education 27
    Education funding 29
    Minority child development 37
    Financial education 43
    Health education 45

Community
    Crime prevention 51
    Culture and heritage 61
    Housing 71
    Recreation 80
    Human relations 86
    Volunteerism 88

Education
    Cultural awareness 95
    Citizenship 98
    Creativity 99
    Family involvement 100
    Young entrepreneurs 103

Environment
    Animals 105
    Biodiversity 110

    Recycling..118
    Sustainability...120

Family
    Parenting...123
    Volunteerism...134
    Work-life balance..137

Health and Wellness
    Chronic illness..141
    Community..148
    Mental health..154
    Disabilities...156

Museums
    Membership...161
    Treasures..163
    Children...164
    Imagination..165
    Management..167

Poverty
    Energy aid..171
    Housing..174

Victim Support
    Children...177
    Security..179
    Lifestyle..181
    Safe communities..183

Women
    Stress relief...185
    Achievement..187
    Health..192
    Networking..195

Index 198

About the Authors 204

Cold Cash for Warm Hearts
101 Best Social Marketing Initiatives

Foreword

As a longtime student of Richard Steckel, I am humbled to have been asked to add a few words of introduction to this important resource. As the foremost leader in earned revenue strategies for nonprofit organizations, Richard is the one who has made it more accessible than anybody else alive. His new book comes at a critically important time. Because of the confluence of several large forces of history, including the projection of massive federal deficits, the budget cuts that are likely to follow, and the reduced assets of many endowed grant makers, nonprofit sustainability depends more than ever before on the capacity of these organizations to create wealth for themselves.

Nonprofits have long experimented with earned revenue strategies. Those with multi-million dollar budgets, as well as organizations with only four or five staff members, are trying their hand at selling products and services to support their mission. Their ventures range from food service to child care, sawmills to sailboats, retail shops to research services. We know from our own experience at Community Wealth Ventures that there is a huge appetite for such strategies in the nonprofit sector, but the number of places to turn for advice on how to do it is extremely limited. Consulting assistance is too expensive for many organizations. And so, a book like Richard's that combines applicability with concrete and practical utility is certain to be received with wild enthusiasm.

One of the most pronounced differences between for-profits and nonprofits is access to capital. As a result, organizations with superior products and services still are challenged when it comes to growing to scale. Richard's ideas show them how to do that. Of the many, many organizations that try this path, most are marginally profitable or break even and only a few have robust profits. The exceptions are often the organizations with which Richard has worked. His deep experience, win-win philosophy, and engaging style have resulted in numerous success stories and "market leaders" that not only thrive but serve as an example for so many other organizations.

The advantages of generating such earned revenues go beyond simply having more resources to execute one's mission. They represent a different kind of resource. Because it is creating new wealth, a community wealth enterprise does not directly compete with other nonprofits for scarce charitable dollars. And most important, revenues generated in this manner have no strings attached. There are no government or foundation regulations that restrict their use. This means an organization can spend such dollars on programs that are not only popular, but also right and necessary (which are not always the same things). Equally important, an organization can choose not to spend such dollars on programs at all, but rather to invest in the operating capacity of the organization. Funds for operating expenses are the most scarce of all, and the most valuable to nonprofits that intend to grow their programs to scale.

Still, the field remains embryonic and in some ways unproven. There are as many failures as successes. For too many ventures the path to profitability cannot be clearly ascertained. Often, the cultures of nonprofit organizations have not adapted to meet their ambition to earn income.

One of the most important ways of advancing the field is not simply through funding and capital but by capturing knowledge and being willing to share it. That is the real generosity of spirit embodied by Richard Steckel–the willingness and commitment to take what is hard learned and to share it so freely that success is not hoarded but rather spread and replicated.

–Billy Shore

Introduction

Creativity fuels every individual and every organization. Sometimes, we need a little creative boost for effect, just as yeast causes a doughy lump to rise into a beautiful loaf of bread. At other times, we need a creative overhaul. These initiatives are offered in service to both of these challenges.

If you have viewed your company or nonprofit organization in the same way year after year, your customers and clients will, too. On the other hand, if you surprise people with an exciting, new marketing initiative they never considered before, everyone can benefit. The "what ifs" multiply as each individual learns about and talks about the change. But, excitement of this kind requires thinking ahead. It starts with considering the cause and effect relationship between creativity and outcomes. It continues with consistent attention to creative thinking. This consistency comes about only through scheduled time out for brainstorming, sharing ideas and learning better ways to think. (Some "thinkers about thinking" who can help in this learning process include Edward de Bono, Roger von Oech and Todd Siler. Their learning resources are widely available in books, video and audio products.)

The staff at AddVenture Network came up with the ideas in this book and they have presented them to hundreds of companies and organizations. Some of the ideas have become a reality and others have not. Regardless, the staff keep coming up with new ideas and do not limit themselves during the process of "ingredient gathering" (brainstorming). Refining, or adding logic to the mix, comes after everyone has contributed a large number of "unleavened" (incomplete) ideas. This expansive approach increases the likelihood that fresh, workable ideas will emerge.

Despite its subtitle, this book contains many hundreds of initiatives, bundled into 101 unifying concepts, or **Ideas**. The ideas are organized by the type and mission of an organization, such as a nonprofit crime prevention agency, a professional nurses association, or a toy manufacturing company. Each idea is described according to its **Strategy**, **Underlying Value**, **Components** and **Execution**. The underlying value of each idea is actually dual in nature; it encompasses value to the organization and value to society. The components and execution offer the meat of each initiative, with innumerable ideas to adopt, adapt, incorporate and connect to business and nonprofit work.

Though many of the ideas contained here are described in the conditional, as if they could happen, many of them have already been carried out successfully by organizations across the world. Since every organization is unique, the reader is encouraged to take this idea yeast and mold marketing initiatives that best match the mission and resources of his or her organization.

Like yeast, ideas take up little space, but they have great power. They can sit on the shelf of our minds for some time before they contribute to an extraordinary event or outcome. It is in this spirit that the reader is invited to read on.

Seniors

Idea 1

Organization: Senior Citizen Service Center
Subject Area: Seniors – Interaction
Keyword Search: senior citizens, community, aging, elder care, mature adults, seniors

Strategy
Establish a program for a senior community center that serves to educate the community on aging adults through interaction. This center should focus on having a positive impact on the participating senior while earning sustainable revenue.

Underlying Value
This program should celebrate aging as a process that makes one wise, reflective and patient. It should also provide the senior with an outlet to share his or her vast experiences and wisdom.

Components

Rent-A-Gramps. The center will contract seniors who are available to individuals, families, organizations and corporations to provide services related to their interests. Examples of potential renters include:
- A day care group that needs a storyteller
- Individuals who need a "sounding board"
- Parents who want their children to spend time with an older, wiser person (regardless of whether or not they have grandparents)
- An organization that wants to revive handicraft arts such as knitting, baking, weaving, tatting, crocheting and canning (the arts that are not being passed down from generation to generation)
- A school administrator who wants to offer students a personal account of historical events or "the good ol' days"
- A family that needs someone with time and patience to help organize family projects such as a stamp or coin collection, photo albums or a home video collection.

Execution

The organization should begin by evaluating the demographic makeup of the seniors the organization serves. To ensure the best participation, it is necessary to make a list of each interested senior's talents, abilities and skills (the "assets" the group possesses) and then determine their availability.

The organization can create a basic marketing tool to sell the Rent-A-Gramps service. This can take the form of a brochure, flyer, email or other form of marketing information. The mission of the service should clearly state where the money generated will go and who will receive the benefits of that revenue. Also, the marketing should detail the hourly or project-based rates and the payment process.

Personal quotes from seniors in the organization will bring life to the marketing materials. One senior may say she loves to knit and has seen this pastime skip the younger generation completely. Or, a World War II veteran may tell how the war changed his life forever, noting that it was more than a historical event, an aspect often overlooked in school lesson plans.

Schools, community centers, houses of worship and other nonprofit organizations are all potential outlets to which the organization can distribute the marketing materials. To kick start interest, the program director should offer to give a presentation or very informal talk about the program.

As services are requested, patterns are established and major areas of interest are defined, product development will be a natural marketing offshoot of the program. Examples include family history tapes, recipe collections and a "how-to" of knitting.

> **Idea 2**
>
> **Organization:** Senior Caregivers Program
> **Subject Area:** Seniors – Comfort
> **Keyword Search:** senior, senior citizen, retiree, care provider, illness

Strategy
Partner with a corporation that provides a product or service for seniors. Invite the corporate partner to join in developing the Comfort and Joy Product Line. Seniors may use this line of products to show recognition and appreciation for caregivers, family members and friends.

Underlying Value
The corporate partner will gain five distinct benefits from an integrated marketing strategy.

- Consumers have one more reason to make purchases from the company–to support the organization while at the same time celebrating the heroism of caregiving.
- Brand equity will be improved for both the corporate name and, where applicable, the family of brands of its subsidiary companies.
- The corporate partner will have more opportunities to effectively launch new products, lift sales of specific products, and generate media attention.
- Increased, measurable profits will be seen at all levels of the corporate structure.
- Customer loyalty will increase.

Because the organization provides one-on-one assistance to seniors by other seniors (primarily the frail elderly who do not live in long-term care facilities), it stands out as an excellent marketing partner. It helps people in need, not people who have experienced a tragedy. This strategy will embody the quality of care, the positive attitude and the practical help this organization delivers.

Components

Comfort and Joy Product Lines. Often, the celebratory value of life's simple pleasures–a warm meal, friendly conversation, a comfortable bed, a kind word–are overlooked. Comfort and Joy is a set of products that reminds us to appreciate these generous acts that caregivers perform.

The Senior Companions Comforter. This downy bedcover would be marketed for its warmth and softness as well as the support its purchase brings to senior companions who bring comfort and joy to elderly clients and their families.

Travel Pillow. This pillow was created to remind the consumer of the comforts of home when traveling. The branded pillow would come with a set of tips on how to avoid illness and injury while traveling.

Small Comforts. This collection of perfumes, soaps and bath oils could be developed using natural products. Small Comforts would include information from the organization on how small comforts can help elderly individuals sustain an independent lifestyle.

Soothing Sunday. This collection would feature "soothing" drinks like iced tea and hot cocoa that appeal to seniors as well as the larger adult population. Patrons would be urged to purchase these drinks one Sunday a month in designated outlets, with proceeds going to the organization.

Execution

The Senior Companions Comforter. The organization can sell comforters through retail locations that are operated by the corporate partner or those of related companies. Through a partnership with a national hotel chain, each bed would be made up with the comforter. At the end of their hotel stay, guests would take the comforter with them and allow the replacement cost to be added to their bill. A portion of that cost would go to Senior Companions.

Travel Pillow. The organization can market this pillow through retail outlets, highlighting not only its familiarity but also the hygienic benefits of air, bus or train travel with one's own pillow.

Small Comforts Perfume. Through a corporate partner's distribution network, the organization can sell these fragrances in gift shops and other retail locations. Consumers can be encouraged to take advantage of a discount and donation rolled into one: buy one, get the second at half price and donate the second Small Comforts purchase to a caregiver who works with the organization. The company would send the donations to the nonprofit partner for distribution to their clientele.

Soothing Sunday. Every Sunday for one month at cafes, taverns, restaurants and leisure facilities nationwide, a corporate partner with interests in these industries would designate fifty percent of all sales of iced tea, hot cocoa or other soothing drinks to the organization. While promoting products that are already marketed as relaxing, this event would also tie the corporate partner to the organization's efforts to soothe its clients.

Idea 3

Organization: Seniors Companion Program
Subject Area: Seniors – Public Garden
Keyword Search: symbolism, logo, senior, aging, care provider, elder, garden path

---

Strategy

Create a symbolic campaign that enhances the organization's mission. Design a symbol to represent the campaign in a way that is similar to other nationally recognized nonprofit organization symbols (such as the AIDS activist's red lapel ribbon or the breast cancer activist's pink ribbon, promoted with the help of Avon).

Underlying Value

With extensive research and exploration, the organization can establish a national symbol affirming caregivers and reinforcing a corporate partner's commitment to this organization.

For millions of people, nothing is more soothing, more cherished than the image of a gently winding walkway through flowers and trees. Some of us would rather spend time in our gardens than just about anywhere else. But for this organization, the garden path is far from private; it is our national garden, our place of common respite and refreshment. It helps us remember the comforts and joys of life and affirm our resolve to make the world a better place. The garden path concept allows the seniors companion program to:
- Identify a quality image shared by most citizens in our society
- Link the image to a common experience, a material possession, or a place that citizens can picture in their minds when they think of the corporate partner and its efforts to serve elderly citizens

- Offer consumers the opportunity to participate in the symbol, giving tangible expression to their experiences of giving or receiving care
- Create a cost effective symbol that can be promoted efficiently without great construction or transportation expense.

Components

The participating corporate partner would purchase or lease a small strip of real estate at a location that invokes elements of our nation's heritage, a community sidewalk close to home and hearts. They would then replace the cement sidewalk with bricks arranged in an attractive pattern, winding their way through a naturally beautiful setting. (Bricks or tiles would set this "place" apart from just another sidewalk.)

Signage and national advertising would encourage passers-by to take a closer look at this path since each brick carries a message. The message might be a "thank you" from a former client to a beloved care provider; a remembrance of a loved one who struggled to retain dignity late in life; or a challenge to one's neighbors to join the fight to establish adequate, affordable quality care for the elderly. For a modest price–with a portion of the cost going directly to the organization–anyone could add a tile to the garden path. Smaller versions of the path could be created in local communities around the country.

Execution

As the program grows, a "Traveling Path" could be developed in the form of a short walkway made up of bricks that can be easily disassembled and moved to other locations.

In addition, all employees of the corporate partner could wear on their lapels a miniature version of the garden path tile. At first glance, a customer might think it is an attractive piece of jewelry, but on closer inspection would likely ask the employee about its meaning. The employee would then have an opportunity to tell that customer or guest, with a sense of pride in ownership, about the company's commitment to the organization and its mission.

Once awareness of the path is established, the organization and its partner could pursue a strategy similar to Avon's pink ribbon. Employees would offer customers the opportunity to buy a lapel-sized tile of their own, with proceeds going back to the organization.

The program and the corporate partner would hold a kick-off event to establish continued awareness of the path and to "pave the way" for subsequent efforts. This would generate two important supports to any new effort: media coverage and a benchmark of public awareness of the company's dedication to affirming caregivers as the true heroes of our society.

> **Idea 4**
>
> **Organization:** National Insurance Provider
> **Subject Area:** Seniors – Volunteerism
> **Keyword Search:** retirement, continued education, job fair, volunteering, senior citizen, active seniors, altruism

Strategy
Build upon the creed many senior citizens live by: Giving service to others is the best way to live out one's sunset years.

Underlying Value
The organization can develop programs or products under an "Improving with Age" concept to promote service by seniors and to seniors. The corporate partner can position the company as a practical resource for information and an enthusiastic advocate for active, altruistic adulthood.

Components
Careers in Caring. Working in partnership with a nonprofit or a group of organizations, the company will offer seniors the opportunity to attend a "job fair." The fair matches their skills and interests with programs and initiatives.

Service Credits. Through this incentive program, the corporate partner can reduce retirement costs, promote sales of specific products and position the company as one that puts its money where its mouth is regarding volunteerism with and by seniors.

Execution
Careers in Caring. The event could be hosted in the corporate partner's retail locations, on their Web site or on an original Web site. Like a college job fair, this event will focus on the valuable skills the nonprofit is seeking.

The difference, of course, is that recruiters will describe the rewards of this work in non-monetary terms, such as pride, self-esteem, problem solving and human relationships.

Service Credits. The corporation's human resources department could own and manage this initiative to encourage employee participation. If this added work causes internal strife, the human resources worker who recruits a specified number of employees to participate should receive an added incentive.

As an internal incentive, those employees approaching retirement can "bank" all of the credits they earn while volunteering for older retirees from the company. Upon retirement, they can cash in these credits for service from another, younger employee. As a promotional vehicle, customers can gain discounts on the purchase of specific items when they bank credits they earn in service to seniors.

Idea 5

Organization: Senior Companion Program
Subject Area: Seniors – Retirement Planning
Keyword Search: senior citizen, aging, corporate sponsorship, financial institutions, communications, caregiver, hero, savings plans, insurance, senior housing

Strategy
Introduce the "Caregiver as Hero" theme to the public through a corporate partner in order to raise awareness and money for the organization's mission.

Underlying Value
The Senior Companion Program is a practical application of the organization's mission to elevate care providers in the community. In addition, it helps the corporate partner gain a strategic advantage–a "Corporate Caring Edge"–in its respective market. This positioning suggests a responsive company that is dedicated to meeting the needs of current and potential customers as well as current and retired employees.

Components
This program will tap into the relationships that the corporate partner has

already established. For example, communication and media outlets can assist in raising awareness. Financial institutions can also assist in creating programs that use savings, insurance, mortgage and other vehicles to trigger income for the organization's cause.

Execution
The corporate partner should place advertisements and send out press releases to cultivate relationships with key individuals who report on elder care issues. All communication should be designed to position the partner and the organization as innovators and advocates for issues that older citizens care about. The largest magazines for this audience in the United States include *AARP Bulletin* and *Modern Maturity*.

A number of financial mechanisms for employees would benefit both the employee and the corporate partner through a mutual investment approach. They would also benefit the companion program by providing long-term stability.

Unused Sick Days. This savings plan allows an employee of the corporate partner to apply the cash value of unused sick days to the elder care insurance policy. This mechanism saves the company money because it provides an incentive to *not* use sick days unnecessarily.

Caring Covenant. This program allows employees who have reached retirement age the opportunity to work part time without threatening access to their retirement benefits. The covenant, an agreement between the corporate partner and retired employee, states that the employer will compensate a still-contributing retired employee with credits rather than cash. These credits, which accumulate until the employee retires, fund access to the services of a senior companion when the retired person or the spouse needs it.

Savings Plans. The corporate partner can match employee contributions to a savings account established specifically to fund personal or family insurance for long-term care, including access to a senior companion. Over a number of years, this account can mature to guarantee a certain number of hours or years that the retired employee (or his or her parent) can have with a senior companion.

A number of financial mechanisms for customers would bring financial support to the program and an increased awareness of the corporate partner's commitment to maintaining a "caring edge."

The Companion Card. This card, free to all customers of the corporate partner, would represent membership in a program similar to a frequent flyer plan. Every purchase from the corporate partner translates into credits earned. The customer can cash the credits in the form of a service the organization offers. In this instance, a senior companion can be hired at no cost. Customer use of the program builds loyalty and increases sales, while triggering corporate donations to the organization.

Lower Cost Insurance Policies. To avoid the frustrating process of finding the best insurance rates, anyone can take out an elder care insurance policy sponsored by the corporate partner. All premiums would go into an insurance pool that the organization can access.

No Place Like Home. This idea, inspired by the Robert Wood Johnson Foundation, ensures independence by extending in-home services to residents in senior housing developments. The foundation focuses on low-income housing finance agencies (HFAs) that offer grants to improve and expand services such as transportation, housekeeping and social workers.

In this social marketing initiative, the corporate partner can expand the foundation's idea. The partner might choose to fund improvement of services to residents in privately-funded housing developments (perhaps where the parents of their consumers or employees live.) These contracts with housing managers would include promotion of the organization's efforts and would publicize the company's dedication to making elder care a high priority.

Children

Idea 6

Organization: Private Family-Oriented Group of Companies
Subject Area: Children – Outdoor Adventure
Keyword Search: scouts, scouting outdoor adventure, youth development, family survival skills, milestones, growth chart, calendar, first aid kit, road safety

Strategy

Develop a values-driven strategic marketing plan that achieves four main objectives for the organization and its corporate partner(s).

- Enhance the company image as the national leader in corporate responsibility
- Create a model for effective partnerships between other businesses and worthy charitable organizations

- Raise the profile of the youth organization, and favorably change its image for better positioning in the coming decades
- Generate substantial income for scouting programs through sales that also build revenue and market share for the company.

Underlying Value

Scouting represents a family of values that the company models in its corporate image. Four initiatives will link the company's products to the scout movement.

- Family Adventure – advocates initiative and leadership and suggests products that help families discover new experiences together, just as scouting encourages young people to explore and "have courage."
- Family Milestones – encourages pride and celebration of family life, linking products to the scouting ethics of trust, loyalty and mutual respect.
- Family Survival Skills – offers practical translation of scouting's vision for resourceful young people who can venture forth from stable, well-equipped families.
- "Be Prepared" – links the scouting theme across subsidiaries of the company through family-branded products. If the company has an existing line of products, this package of products can be sold through its current network of sales systems. They would not require new product development schemes.

Components

Family Adventure Calendar. This annual, multi-purpose product features scouts and their families engaging in fun activities. It is packed with stickers to celebrate the date (or anniversary) of adventures pursued by the scout's family, directions on how to get to certain places, checklists of supplies needed for outdoor fun, and coupons for the company's family-branded products such as lanterns, batteries, waterproof clothing and compasses. In addition, families have an opportunity to participate.

Families could also be encouraged to submit stories of their own adventures for the next year's calendar with tips or warnings to ensure a safe and enjoyable outing.

Family Milestones Growth Chart. This product includes hints for families, such as dealing with peer pressure, or how parents can help children conquer minor battles like nail biting. It lists helpful products (all available at company stores) for different ages, such as teething remedies, school supplies, or treatments for acne. The chart would encourage and help celebrate a young person's internal and physical growth. It would also include a perforated section of detachable coupons. For example, a coupon could offer a discount on specific products when a child reaches a certain number of inches in height.

Smart Families Safety Kit. Scouting is a valuable way for a company to market household safety products, everything from reflective clothing and bicycle locks to torches and alarm systems. This kit would actually be a catalogue, featuring scouts using the items with their parents. The kit would include a checklist of family safety strategies like "preparing a fire escape plan" and "following a safe route home from school." In addition, it would give examples of how families can work together to build a sense of unity and mutual concern. The kit would also include coupons, redeemable at company stores, for products that are featured in the catalogue.

Be Prepared Road Safety Kit. Available at the company's convenient store locations, this kit would include family-branded motor oil, flares and road maps, along with scout compasses and a space blanket. Company-branded lanterns, emergency radios and branded snacks and supplies could also be featured.

Be Prepared First Aid Kit. Available at the company's drug stores, the kit would include family-branded bandages, antiseptics and over-the-counter medical products (such as antacids). It would also contain the company's branded antibacterial soap, a family emergency preparedness video, and scouting-branded products such as snake bite treatments, pocket knives and tourniquets.

The Be Prepared kits are useful beyond a scouting or youth development context, but there is always a logical link to that context.

Execution

Advertising Opportunities. Using existing advertising budgets, the company will reinforce its image as a family-oriented group of companies that is innovative and attractive. The ads will present a similar image of scouting. Part of the challenge in breaking old stereotypes of scouting as outdated and unattractive is to replace those judgments with more positive qualities. An exciting advertising campaign would feature company stores and products in the context of a new message: "And You Thought Otherwise."

This ad campaign would blast the image of awkward children engaged in far-fetched activities (marching, saluting or just reading the scout handbook) and replace it with the "real" image of scouting: kids in the inner city, designing and building a playground. Another ad might feature strong, vital-looking rural youth orienting themselves, using compasses, telescopes and sophisticated electronic positioning equipment. Each of these visuals would feature many of the products marketed under the company program with an announcement that they are available at one of the company's family stores.

Delivery Program. Instead of the age-old image of a scout helping the elderly woman across the street, the company can create an image of the new generation of scouts by establishing a home delivery program. When a large item is purchased (such as twenty-five pounds of fertilizer), a scout could deliver it to someone's home for an extra cost.

Mini-Stores. This "store within a store" promotion would occupy an area with unique signage, displays that are designed differently from others in the store, and its own cash registers. Employees trained to sell scouting-branded products would wear a lapel button announcing "Company X Loves Scouting." The mini-store would only carry products directly related to the company relationship.

Scouts might serve as volunteers at a mini-store for a few hours on Saturdays. They would be engaged in typical scouting activities, presenting an image of scouting that a typical shopper might not expect. Groups of friendly, enthusiastic youth designing a computer program or tinkering with a mountain bike would refresh the public's image of scouts and increase the value of nearby products.

Vendor Cooperation. Vendors concerned with marketing their own brand can participate with the company and scouting organizations to further increase the value of the partnership. A campaign might feature the following: "During National Scout Week, Company X will designate ten percent of all proceeds from the sale of camping lanterns to the scouting organization, and Corporation Y will match that amount to further support the company efforts on behalf of scouting."

Children / 19

Organization: Youth Advocacy Organization
Subject Area: Children – Advocacy
Keyword Search: child development, family welfare, child care centers, kids club, play

Strategy
Reposition the youth advocacy organization as a cutting edge program provider and a national resource center for corporations while diversifying its income sources.

Underlying Value
Knowing that talented employees come at a price, which includes the holistic provision for their families, companies strive to provide services that support the employee's efforts. The organization can address these concerns from a long-standing history of developing and supporting programs and services for families.

Components
Direct Services to Corporations. The organization can offer programs and advice in setting up systems for working families. Corporations would "buy" an employee benefit or family support package that is customized to meet the needs of the corporation and its employees.

Child Development and Care Centers. This center (or centers, if multiple corporate locations are involved) is designed by the organization. The corporation supports it (investment memberships) by providing access for their employees at a reduced or preferred service rate. Or, it can be added to the options in the employee benefit packages.

Playspaces. These play areas for children can be offered as a direct benefit to employees in the corporate environment, or for the general public in a community location such as an airport or shopping mall. It would be sold to the appropriate location concerns, such as the mall development corporation or airline.

Playspaces would provide resource rooms with age grouping of toys. Also, a family bulletin board would feature child development news and information. Local businesses and nonprofit organizations would provide a list or current schedule of their activities, along with everything from parenting workshops, museum exhibits and sports teams to "family friendly" hotels and restaurants.

Execution

Direct Services to Corporations. The organization can offer a range of services, such as setting up the administrative structure and guidelines for an on-site day care center, or training existing staff to provide quality services for families. The earned income as a fee for service would have a profit built in for unrestricted use by the nonprofit.

As the nonprofit builds its reputation as the credible, experienced child care provider in that community, its corporate customers would benefit, too. Their on-site day care centers would attract employees who seek the best for their children.

Child Development and Care Centers. As a service to the general public, the school would develop centers for child development and child care in cooperation with the staff and administration of medical facilities. The centers would provide "sick child" day care, developmental testing, and therapy for certain families. Designed in cooperation with health facilities, the organization and care centers may be eligible for third party payment options.

Playspaces. All of the organization's affiliated programs would include a quality control system built into the pricing of the package, allowing the organization to periodically evaluate programs and services to ensure compliance with their defined national standards. The organization's development centers, kids clubs and playspaces would evolve as national resources for professional child care training. This would including training for day care providers and national internship opportunities for child development and education students.

Idea 8

Organization: Nonprofit Foster Care Provider
Subject Area: Children – Advocacy
Keyword Search: foster care, teens, conflict resolution, parenting skills, transition, child welfare

Strategy

Effectively position the organization among nonprofit organizations and raise its profile for a broader class of constituents. Move outside the "social work paradigm" by pursuing innovative sources of funding for the organization's projects. And, increase the focus on quality of life for children after they leave the care system.

Underlying Value

This organization has a long and successful history of working with youth in foster care as they transition from children to adults without the benefit of a permanent family. Recognizing this knowledge as a valuable asset, the organization can help a corporation:

- Help create responsible citizens among the next generation of adults
- Understand the "millennium mindset" and effectively market to teens, a dramatically influential segment of consumers
- Teach employees and customers valuable life skills in the important areas of parenting, friendship and coping with change
- Help provide children with a sense of stability in the world whether they are in the system or out, while also building self-esteem for the teenage years and helping them adopt valuable traditions that will improve their future parenting styles.

Components

This initiative helps prepare children to be good citizens by giving their parents access to essential child rearing tools. This positions the organization and its corporate partner as tremendous resources for information, training and development of skills such as:

- Managing conflict effectively
- Improving communication between parent and child
- Helping children through difficult social situations
- Remaining resilient in the face of rapid change
- Modeling responsible citizenship.

Execution

Parenting Kiosks. The kiosk communicates parenting advice that was developed by experts at the organization. It captures parents' attention while they wait in airports, train stations, college student unions and office building lobbies. Free-standing stations with computer touch screens would allow visitors to ask questions and search for information about making positive personal choices for the benefit of their children.

The visitor would follow prompts on the screen. A printer inside the kiosk would generate information, free of charge, as a take-away. The corporate partner has a "captive audience" in this concept, plus an opportunity to promote its products on each printout.

Parenting Power Digital Dialogues. This online opportunity allows the public to ask celebrities questions about preparing for parenting in the modern world. Celebrity participants could include individuals who successfully grew up in the care system, or entertainers who thoroughly understand and can communicate the key role that positive parenting plays in the lives of their young fans. This "event" could be linked to both the corporate partner and nonprofit partner Web sites to broaden the audience.

Family Conflict Indicator. This chart, book, calendar or poster would alert parents to "early warning signs" of harmful conflict and describe techniques to disarm and prevent escalating family violence. The indicator would answer the questions: "What types of conflict are productive?" "What feelings are absorbed with positive conflicts?" and "What are the signs of verbal and emotional abuse?" Because corporations like practical, inexpensive products that effectively communicate a social message, this one would appeal to a broad range of potential partners.

Bully-Proofing and other Good Ideas Booklets. This product could be offered for sale or as a premium with the purchase of a product. These sets of guidelines teach parents how to help with specific social situations such as how to deal with a bully or a difficult authority figure, how to be assertive rather than aggressive, or how to share. As the experts at this organization know, many young people do not grow to parenthood with good role models for dealing with difficult and painful social issues. This product's practical strategies help them become role models who support their children through the rocky road to adulthood.

Parent Sabbaticals. The vast majority of parents want to do a good job with their children, but the heavy demands of everyday life often make self-improvement a low priority. This weekend away at a hotel or resort includes seminars on topics such as effectively managing conflict, improving communication and helping children through difficult social situations. It also provides a good dose of rest and relaxation, sending the parents home with a better frame of mind to take on the challenges of modern child-rearing. This would interest a hotel chain as a way to increase traffic on the weekends.

Family Milestones and Memorabilia Kit. This set of products is designed to help parents understand the importance of memories, shared experiences and special occasions to the healthy development of children. It could contain photo albums with suggestions for events to include, a growth chart, and a timeline to record important life passages and transitions. Businesses could add their support to this product by offering discount coupons for items like a construction kit to make a dog house for the new pet or make-up for a girl's first formal dance.

Idea 9

Organization: Nonprofit Foster Care Provider
Subject Area: Children – Advocacy
Keyword Search: foster care, transition, youth, technology, teens, pen pals, gift registry, consulting services

Strategy

Position the organization among nonprofits and raise its profile for a broader class of constituents. Move outside the "social work paradigm" by pursuing innovative funding methods. And, increase the focus on quality of life for children after they leave the care system.

Underlying Value

This organization has a long and successful history of working with youth as they transition from children to adults without the benefit of a permanent family. Recognizing this valuable knowledge asset, the provider can help a corporation:
- Create a well-prepared workforce for the 21st Century
- Understand the "millennium mindset" and effectively market to teens, a dramatically influential segment of consumers
- Teach employees and customers valuable life skills in the important areas of parenting, friendship and coping with change.

Components

Teens know technology. Today, they use it more than ever for communication, recreation and education. There is no better way to reach this population than through their familiar computer environment. The staff at the organization also knows a lot about technology and the trends that influence teens. Their expertise can come in handy as they work with a corporate sponsor to create technology and Internet-based products and services.

Execution

TNT Consulting Service. This online service gives the company the opportunity to inform the marketplace that it understands marketing to young consumers. A set of manuals would be available for sale to other companies on topics such as how to treat teen consumers and how to hire and keep quality teen employees. This online service would allow companies to pay a membership fee for access to survey results gathered by the organization as well as their expert opinions on teen consumer behavior.

Internet Pen Pals. While the Internet offers a number of opportunities for the organization and its marketing partner to promote their efforts, this one is of particular interest because it would offer youth the chance to communicate via email with a young person in another city. The organization would suggest questions that participants can ask one another, and perhaps help kids who live in stable families better understand the challenges of a young person who is being looked after in the care system. Every time a teen signs on the Pen Pal Program, he or she would see messages promoting the corporate sponsor's products. Income for the partnership would be generated from advertising for non-competing products or services placed in the online software used for Internet Pen Pals.

Teen Gift Registries. Retail corporations are quickly discovering that bridal and baby gift registries have great potential for expansion. Children can go to a toy store and key into a handheld computer the products they would like to receive for their birthday or a holiday. Recent graduates could do the same for gift items needed for a new apartment or for their first term at a university. This positions the organization as the one that knows what kids want as well as what they need to succeed in the future.

Together with their retail partners or e-commerce partners on the Internet, the organization would provide lists of various types of products to registered teens who can choose what they like, then pass the list on to potential gift-givers. The organization can also provide its marketing partner with percentages indicating most and least favored products, teen feedback and other information that improves selling efforts to these consumers.

Children / 25

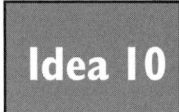

Organization: Foster Care Provider
Subject Area: Children – Advocacy
Keyword Search: youth, character development, life skills development, financial education

Strategy
Effectively position the organization among nonprofit organizations and raise its profile for a broader class of constituents. Move outside the "social work paradigm" by pursuing innovative sources of funding for the organization's projects. And, increase the focus on quality of life for children after they leave the care system.

Underlying Value
This organization has a long and successful history of working with youth as they transition from children to adults without the benefit of a permanent family. Recognizing this valuable knowledge asset, the provider can help a corporation:
- Create a well-prepared workforce for the 21st Century
- Understand the "millennium mindset" and effectively market to teens, a dramatically influential segment of consumers
- Teach employees and customers valuable life skills in the important areas of parenting, friendship and coping with change.

Components
Because it works closely with children, this organization is in a position to evaluate whether a young person has the tools to become a quality member of the modern workforce. This group of products and services positions the organization and its corporate partner as a valuable resource for information, training and opportunities to acquire skills such as:
- Traditional and technological literacy
- Developing good work habits
- Managing personal finances effectively
- Setting career goals

- Communicating effectively
- Understanding the needs of employers
- Understanding one's role as a citizen in the community.

Execution

Gotta Get Ready Booklets. Each booklet would address a character issue that is critical to success in the modern workplace. These guides for preparing for the future world of work would promote the skills teens need to get along with others. The series of booklets would be pre-sold to corporations with a reputation for hiring young workers. They would be distributed free of charge via schools, job training services and social welfare organizations. Topics could include:
- Honesty
- Integrity
- Dependability
- Respect for co-workers
- Respect for customers
- A love of learning
- Resilience during change

Managing My Money Clubs. Some of the most common questions raised by teens involve money. In addition, children served by a foster system like this organization find out when they reach working age that they have no idea how to budget, how to open and manage accounts, or how to plan and invest for the future.

Membership in an "M and M" would provide young adults with an opportunity to access information and assistance with financial issues. While not essential, the corporate partners could market products relevant to these financial concerns. Young consumers will be grateful for a resource to help them through an increasingly complex, material world filled with temptations and distractions.

Literacy Mentors. The workers of tomorrow will need both kinds of literacy: traditional and technological. Corporations would purchase the Literacy Mentors subscription service for their young employees. It would provide in-person communication sessions (particularly for those who cannot read or need to read at a higher level). It could also provide telephone assistance and online resources.

Volunteer mentors would be screened by the organization and trained in providing step-by-step instruction to overcome the learning obstacles that have been identified. This allows young workers to advance more quickly and gain more confidence in their abilities, so the corporation procures a more productive workforce.

Youth Enterprise Fairs. The organization and its partner would hold an annual fair at strategic locations throughout the country. These fairs would resemble trade shows where businesses would exhibit information about their products and young people would be encouraged to present their ideas for new businesses. Corporations would be given the opportunity to invest in youth enterprise ideas with a percentage paid (finder's fee) to the sponsoring corporation and the organization.

Other businesses could offer teens discounts on their products as a reward for participating in the fair. These fairs could also present awards for the best new ideas, encouraging young people to believe in themselves and develop a sound business plan.

Idea 11

Organization: Private School
Subject Area: Children – Business Education
Keyword Search: private school, children, education, entrepreneur, small business owner, moneymaking, lemonade stand

Strategy

Launch a special education, potentially moneymaking project for a private school that serves to educate children on concrete business practices and the inner workings of commercial enterprise.

Underlying Value

Children learn best by doing. Running a business will teach them how a business works. This program enables kids to have a practical learning experience funded by a corporate sponsor. The partner gains an enhanced image in the community and increased public awareness of its products and services.

"The Great American Lemonade Stand" projects success. Persuasion is not necessary since a captive market already exists. The merchants (students), product (lemonade) and consumers (easily defined groups) have already been tested. Children have sold lemonade for years because it works. Consumers love the convenience as well as helping kids in their business endeavors, and lemonade is a popular drink.

Components

With a corporate partner's seed money, the organization can create The Great American Lemonade Stand packet. This innovative information packet would include a starter kit, the stand itself, and a multi-level guidebook for setting up a new business. The guidebook would be included as a teaching tool within the packet, which would also feature a colorful mixture of suggestions and business essentials such as:
- The history of lemonade
- Stand construction (an opportunity to personalize the stand)
- Promotion and advertising tips (PR)
- Selling techniques that work
- Management
- Hiring and firing practices
- Organizational management
- Lemonade jokes
- Budgets and record keeping
- Setting goals (sales, profits, construction)
- Competitive pricing.

Execution

The organization would approach a corporate partner to provide venture money to the school. A development team in the organization would then create the educational model or prototype, which would, upon corporate approval, be sold to nonprofit organizations. Both the school and the nonprofits that purchase the kit stand to gain from the venture, both educationally and financially. A portion of each organization's profits could then be funneled to a charitable organization associated with or sponsored by the corporate partner.

Idea 12

Organization: Private Corporation – Convenience Store Franchise, Packaged Goods
Subject Area: Children – Education
Keyword Search: children, parent-teacher association (PTA), parent-teacher organization (PTO), school bonds, store franchise

Strategy

Redefine a corporation's public image to represent one company, one vision and one strategy that can be summed up in a public purpose marketing program called "Values with Value." This phrase will come to reflect a company that stands by its values and simultaneously provides customers with attractive value.

Underlying Value

The corporate partner gains several opportunities to make a lifelong difference in kids' lives by partnering with parents in practical ways around a powerful emotional concern. Positive character development can be effectively addressed through programs with the local PTA or PTO.

Components

The Corporate Champion of Parent-Teacher Associations/Organizations. After the family and sometimes the church and schools are most responsible for positive character development since they provide the tools to ensure success in our society. Parents learn quickly that they have a vitally important relationship with teachers, yet both participants in that relationship can easily be discouraged by their shared challenge. There is never enough money to provide the level of education parents and teachers want for our nation's youth.

The company can leverage these existing relationships to build a powerful alliance with local PTAs or PTOs and their national representatives. It would expand the sales potential for its products and increase parent participation in creating financial support for their schools.

Execution

The corporate partner would position itself as a promoter of parent-teacher cooperative efforts. It would benefit from the group promoting it as a national champion of this essential cornerstone of thousands of schools across the country. Store displays would announce local school news and suggest ways for the public to get involved with local education events. Coupon inserts, hanging tags and store entrances would announce opportunities to become a member of the PTA or PTO in that community. Discounts could also be offered to individuals who join the local group.

The Snack Shop Strategy. The company could also designate certain store products for sale in the school bookstore, cafeteria or snack shop with the understanding that a portion of each sale stays with administrators to fund school projects. The company might also eventually develop a private label brand, one that is sold in snack shops solely to benefit local schools.

For schools without a snack shop, or simply to further the company's message in this concept, a mobile and branded cart could be transported to schools. Students would look forward to the weekly appearance of the company cart, knowing that new items that benefit their own school might be available.

School Bonds. The company would design school bonds as a product item in their store or product line. Customers would buy them in designated increments as part of a shopping trip. At the cash register, the cost of the bonds would be added to the shopper's bill. Each bond sold represents a direct donation to the school with no profit to the retailer. In this way, the company makes support of local schools a simple choice.

Scholarship Contest. Every purchase of a company product would include an entry card for an annual education promotion, the chance to win a university scholarship. Winners would have to maintain a certain grade point average and school attendance record, which increases the likelihood that the award would go to a good steward of this opportunity. Every time a customer shops, he or she gains an additional statistical advantage for his or her child, godchild, grandchild or favorite neighbor. The customer also knows that a donation from that product purchase goes to the local parent-teacher association. Because every entry card represents an actual purchaser, it is a great resource for the company's mailing list.

> **Idea 13**
>
> **Organization:** Private Company – Convenience Store Franchise, Packaged Goods
> **Subject Area:** Children – Education
> **Keyword Search:** children, environmental issues, education, recycling

Strategy

Redefine a corporation's public image to represent one company, one vision and one strategy that can be summed up in a public purpose marketing program called "Values with Value." This phrase will come to reflect a company that stands by its values and simultaneously provides customers with attractive value.

Underlying Value

The corporate partner gains several opportunities to make a lifelong difference in kids' lives by partnering with parents in practical ways around a powerful emotional concern. Programs that effectively address positive character development challenge kids to stand up for the earth that they will inherit. Often, what motivates participation in conservation and recycling programs is our fear of what an abused and deteriorating earth could be like for the next generation. A proposed program to confront that concern is called "Company X and Recycling in Schools: Helping Children Make the Earth a Better Place."

Components

NJC: Not Just Cans. Through shelf talkers, in-store promotions and communication vehicles (such as *Club Card* magazine), the company can remind a customer of items that have recycling potential. Most consumers feel well educated if they know to save aluminum cans, newspapers and glass; very few know how much of an impact they can really have. A bright, colorful NJC tag could educate customers on products that are tied in some way to recycling. Similar information could be distributed to schools, where organized NJC efforts could help generate funding for local education.

Clothing Recycling. If the company has a clothing line, it could follow the example of children's clothing line Hanna Andersen. This catalogue company has told its customers, "If your child outgrows it and it is still in good shape, send it back to us for a credit on your next purchase." Consumers have responded very enthusiastically. They appreciate the opportunity to pass perfectly usable clothing on to another child and to get a discount on new products. Every month, up to four thousand articles of clothing are recycled with Hanna Andersen.

Toy Trade. Similar to the clothing recycling idea, the company would encourage children and families to recycle a toy through a number of mechanisms. This teaches them about generosity, kindness and compassion.

Execution

NJC: Not Just Cans. In order to involve kids in the effort, each company store would offer children special benefits for managing their family's or their neighborhood's recycling efforts. NJC stickers, lapel pins, caps and backpacks would be awarded for achieving certain goals. NJC is also an opportunity to involve employees. An employee could make presentations at local schools, encouraging kids to participate in recycling efforts.

Clothing Recycling. Besides collecting its own used clothing, the company could collect recyclable clothing at schools, providing another mechanism for generating income for local education. In addition, clothing recycling offers the company a way to help educate children about caring for the earth. Hanging tags on children's clothing would demonstrate for kids how their outgrowing a jumper or pair of shoes can be–in the big picture of environmental responsibility–a good thing.

The company may choose to publicize where the recycled clothing has been delivered–places such as domestic violence shelters or inner city day care centers. Children would learn that their participation in the re-use program is not only good for the earth but also good for someone else.

Toy Trade. A simple in-store and in-school promotion for the Toy Trade would invite kids to give away an unneeded toy via a box in the local company store. In return, they would receive a discount on favorite store items such as ice cream or candy. Families could also be encouraged, through discounts, to buy two of a new toy then give one away.

Promotion materials could tell the life story of a special toy, such as a teddy bear (one that is gender-neutral and not very age specific). The booklet would tell how Bear was made and how he or she got to the local store. After being loved by the boy or girl who buys this toy, Bear is then recycled for use by another child. Children would learn that their generous donation of Bear brings comfort to a child in need. They would also learn that their donation can make a difference for the environment.

Idea 14

Organization: Private Company – Grocery Store, Packaged Goods, Franchised Convenience Store
Subject Area: Children – Education
Keyword Search: children, personal growth, diversity, parents, education, values, learning

Strategy
Redefine a corporation's public image to represent one company, one vision and one strategy that can be summed up in a public purpose marketing program called "Values with Value." This phrase will come to reflect a company that stands by its values and simultaneously provides customers with attractive value.

Underlying Value
Not all public purpose efforts have to be serious despite their serious–and worthy–message. The importance of developing certain positive character traits in our children is no exception. This initiative will send the message: "Have Fun with Company X (and Become a Better Person, Too!)" The activities, designed for both fun and personal growth, will promote positive character development. It affords the corporate partner several opportunities to make a lifelong difference in kids' lives by partnering with parents in practical ways around a powerful emotional concern.

Components
The Learning Passport. Like adults, kids love to feel that they are getting a good deal. The Company Y Learning Passport is a product that parents can purchase at a bargain price. It features discounts on tickets to activities children enjoy. Along with passes to the zoo or museum, there might also be fun activities such as a puppet theater or movie houses. Purchase of the product not only represents an educational opportunity for the child but also a donation to local schools.

Kids on the Go. This booklet series would be for sale in company stores. The series features travel guides written by and for children. (They might also be given away as a premium with a purchase.) Children would learn the value of seeing the world and the beautiful diversity of people and languages. They would also gain pride in their own school and community and value the good things about their surroundings. This unique and entertaining education project teaches children good research and composition skills.

Kids on the World Wide Web. Again, in partnerships with schools, the company could create an Internet home page to communicate with children and their parents about educational, creative and practical ideas for having fun and making a positive difference their world.

Execution

The Learning Passport: A Role for Company Suppliers. Vendors can sponsor specific passport activities or enhance others. Beverage suppliers and sweets wholesalers can offer discounts on their products in conjunction with a movie house coupon. Camera batteries and film could be offered at a discount when the Learning Passport owner uses a zoo admission coupon. The opportunities for partnership are numerous.

The Learning Passport can also be an educational tool. Specific activities could be featured on take-away cards on display in company stores. These cards would become pages in the passport. The zoo discount might be accompanied by a description of how kids can help save endangered species of animals.

A movie pass, for example, could provide an opportunity to develop generosity. The passport coupons for movie passes could be donated at a company store for kids who cannot afford a trip to see the latest action hero or the newest family adventure film.

In-store displays would promote both the passport concept and its ability to encourage positive character traits in our children. A variation would be to offer "Treat Seats," free discount coupons to local events that are available only by coming to the local company store. A Treat Seats display, as other companies have discovered, is a big traffic builder. It also attracts parents with the promise that the company will offer savings only on quality activities for children and their families.

Kids on the Go. Through advertising and in-store displays, the company would communicate to parents and teachers the multiple value of a Kids on the Go project. Every community with a company store would be eligible for employee volunteers and modest financial support from the company to develop a local Kids on the Go effort. As the sponsor at a primary school, the company would encourage students to communicate what they like to do most in their own towns or cities. From these responses, the company could create a Kids on the Go series and make it available in any store. Families planning a trip to a specific location would get a "kids point of view" on entertaining activities they will find there.

Kids on the World Wide Web. Children would help write the text for the Web site and post photos of children participating in recycling programs. Kids on the Go research or interesting family activities would complement the concept. Needless to say, the home page would also target store customers of all demographic segments, relaying information about Values with Value promotions.

Idea 15

Organization: Private School
Subject Area: Children – Education
Keyword Search: private school, parenting, international understanding, youth enterprise, scholar, child development

Strategy
Position a private academy as an upbeat, proactive, national pacesetter in education. Accomplish this by establishing nationally prominent centers for international understanding and youth enterprise.

Underlying Value
The private school is at a unique advantage because its programs represent global awareness in concrete form. Every day, they put into practice the principles that promote greater understanding of and appreciation for cultural diversity through their student body, faculty and course content. And, the opportunity to produce corporate, educator and general public ventures for international understanding is timely, given today's tensions.

Components

Expanding its programs and educational content to new locations, times and audiences allows the academy to broaden its base while enhancing its image as the provider of an educational experience a person cannot find anywhere else. The school would fund these aggressive programs using both a traditional method and a less conventional earned income method that capitalizes on parent and alumni gifts. A director of enterprise or business development position would be created. This person (who reports directly to the school administration) would spearhead the financial initiatives by monitoring all aspects of the academy's development.

Execution

International School Curriculum. This curriculum could double as a service and a product; it would include seminars and training for teachers and parents. The curriculum would be based on knowledge that the school has garnered over the years about how to teach kids from over one hundred nations from an international perspective. Additionally, it could help achieve this goal with products that may already be a part of the school's daily curriculum. By being the first to provide the curriculum, it establishes the school as the international standard.

Scholar in Residence. Each year, the academy would bring in an internationally known writer, playwright, artist, philosopher, economist or other leader to teach classes and workshops on a regular basis with students, faculty and parents. Evening sessions could be open to the general public for an admission fee. If underwritten by a corporation, this could become the "Corporation X Scholar in Residence Program." The public relations and income potential are high, as the corporate partner aligns its image with both new advances and timeless themes.

International Audio Library. The international school could develop this library as a business or community service. Audio recordings could be produced in various languages that are important to businesses that wish to become familiar with a particular culture. Children's level learning materials are useful to those new to a foreign culture. These recordings could be rented out or membership could be available for a fee.

Kids Ports. This idea comes from the Denver Children's Museum but is very appropriate for an international school. The museum opened up a mini-museum in the airport for children who are waiting for arrivals, departures and connecting planes. The international school could enter into a contract with a museum like the Denver Children's Museum or others to maintain a presence in international airports. The exhibits could be thematic: language, geography, environment, or travel, for example.

Center for Youth Enterprise. This program addresses a global economy that is in constant transition. It could explore the concept of a fair and equitable economic system, and feature several initiatives, including:

- School X International Business Enterprise Forum. The school could invite kids to share their business ideas in an open forum. A bank could partner with the school to award seed money to the child with the "best" idea.
- The (Really) Small Business Administration. The school could partner with a bank to offer below-market rate loans for a small amount (like five hundred dollars) to children who go through a planning stage to create a small business. Only young children would qualify.

Idea 16

Organization: African American Child Care Provider and Research Center
Subject Area: Children – Minority Child Development
Keyword Search: children, African American education, positive self-esteem, family relationships

Strategy

With a corporate partner, create a package of products called "A Positive Sense of Self" that promotes a positive self-image in African American children ages seven and younger. Connect the corporation with African American consumers, especially young families, to strengthen their competitive advantage in the marketplace.

Underlying Value

For many years, this organization has recognized the strong relationship between a positive sense of self–including ethnic pride–and a reduction in violent behavior. Good self-esteem is also associated with improved family relationships.

Components

All products under this strategy, whether they are designed to be used or worn, should focus on the child. Adjunct materials can be included to help parents in their work of building the child's self-esteem. Specific attention can be given to acknowledging African American heritage and providing positive connections to the child's racial and cultural roots.

Execution

Cut-Out Books. These books would include paper figurines in modern and historical dress. The text would help children understand the significance of significant characters in African American history or contemporary society. Cut-out or punch-out pages could feature African villages and modern environments. Other activities, such as coloring, games and puzzles, could also be featured.

Sticker Sets. Stickers are ideal because they can portray heroes, heroines, leaders and historical figures through illustrations or photographs. Individual stickers can be included as incentives for good behavior or tools for encouraging a positive sense of self. They can also be sold as part of an activity book that invites the child to place stickers on pages that portray important African American scenes and historical events.

Comic Books. These comics would not feature superheroes; they would tell the stories of real life African American heroes. Stories could highlight historical events such as the March on Washington, or the discoveries of famous scientists and inventors like George Washington Carver, or they could tell of the heroic acts of less famous individuals.

African Folk Tale Video and Audio Series. Aimed at educators and parents, this series of tapes would celebrate African stories for children. The organization can separate itself from the competition by developing a branded series targeted for African American children. These resources would be spoken, musical, live action or animated, and narrators would be famous, contemporary African Americans. The corporate partner could use this as a direct marketing piece to its consumers. In addition, these audio and video recordings can be sold as premiums for cable television companies to motivate subscription renewals. It could also be designed for institutional use at libraries, Head Start locations and schools.

Calendar. This practical product highlights African American concerns and comes illustrated with beautiful African and African American images. The calendar would feature African American organizations and ways that families can join them or make use of their services. It can also include perforated discount coupons for products or services offered by the corporate partner(s). Every month a different theme such as food, music or traditional dress can celebrate a dimension of the rich heritage that African Americans share.

Children's Cookbook. Cooking is a great way for children to learn about cultural heritage. It is also a classic self-esteem builder since it encourages creativity and productivity. Children learn about their ancestors by smelling the same smells, tasting the same flavors and learning how these foods were once prepared. The cookbook can also describe holidays, tell stories or suggest games associated with certain foods.

Idea 17

Organization: African American Child Development Center
Subject Area: Children – Minority Child Development
Keyword Search: African American, communication skills, family preservation, conflict resolution

Strategy

Become recognized as a child development center that provides quality care for African American children while serving the families and communities of these children.

Underlying Value

The center can develop resources for African American families that are suffering under tremendous societal pressures. Its staff has both the professional training and the close contact with families that bring a deep understanding of the needs of these families. Expanding its services will enhance the public's perception of the center as a valuable community resource and create new revenue sources.

Components

Family Preservation. Building strong communication skills is a proven success factor in strengthening the family unit. The center can develop a package of products that encourages healthy communication patterns and problem solving in general, but also address the stressors that are unique to the contemporary African American family.

Execution

Solutions WarmLine. When we think of "hotline" we think of crisis. This service would help families before situations intensify to a crisis level. Through the miracle of touch-tone telephones, callers would access information or handle common family problems. All of the WarmLine ideas would be practical, providing realistic actions that any family can take. A corporate partner such as a telephone company could sell this toll call or offer it free as a public service. This valuable partnership opportunity represents a cost-effective way to use existing technology, generate revenue, and link the corporate partner's service "connections" with family "connectedness."

Cultural Sensitivity Software. This software could be developed for distribution in the corporate partner's retail outlets and as a tool for educators to promote cultural sensitivity among all students. The partner and organization can work together to get the software placed in the local school system. And, if the partner is a computer manufacturer, the software can be given to the African American consumer as a bonus for purchasing the computer.

Greeting Cards. This dual purpose concept offers practical, culturally appropriate products to families. Simple, age-appropriate cards would feature birthday and holiday greetings, party invitations and friendship messages. Caring cards would communicate messages like "Let's talk it out" or "I care about you," and feature pictures of daily family life. The back of each card would feature the center's suggestions for handling conflict or sharing feelings. While purchased as gifts, the cards would carry the additional benefit of educating both the giver and receiver.

Conflict Management Software. This educational software teaches practical family life skills such as conflict management in the context of African American families. It presents an excellent opportunity for a software company seeking improved sales among African Americans.

Family Coping Assessment. Very few Americans feel capable of assessing the seriousness of the problems their families face. This tool, designed by and for African American families, would help adults "take the pulse" of their unique situation. The center would develop it in cooperation with its professional team of psychologists, sociologists and pediatricians, all of whom share a special sensitivity to the needs of African American families. Parents would be able to assess which problems are manageable and which ones require professional intervention to avoid traumatic consequences. The assessment would also direct users to resource materials for improving certain situations. It could be marketed as an annual "check-up," a product that families should invest in every year to assess their emotional and spiritual health and the quality of their communication.

This product could easily be made available through the partner (such as a social service agency, the psychology department of a university, the pediatric ward of a hospital or a counseling center that serves African American families). A corporate partner, such as a pharmaceutical distributor, could create an "in-store" display where African American families can pick up the assessment at no charge, then mail it to the organization for a free analysis.

Idea 18

Organization: African American Child Development Center
Subject Area: Children – Minority Child Development
Keyword Search: children, conflict resolution, prevention, positive self-esteem, domestic violence, child abuse

Strategy
Become recognized as a child development center that provides quality care for African American children and serves the families and communities of these children.

Underlying Value
The center is uniquely qualified to address conflict resolution and violence prevention in African American families. This integrated marketing and educational initiative will establish it as the premier education and training resource for these essential family skills.

Components

The center can partner with a corporation that already sells a product that is appealing to children in general and wants to target the African American consumer in particular. A candy company, toy company, educational resource provider or cinema complex are all potential partners. In addition, the center can create tools that achieve three things:
- Help build self-esteem in young children
- Help families increase healthy functioning
- Give specific advice and techniques for handling conflict that escalates to violence.

Execution

How Kids See Violence. This book/video combination can be marketed to parents and teachers who need tools for teaching children how to avoid violent behavior in themselves and others. Before concerned adults can help children with these skills, they must first understand how children perceive conflict and violence. The organization would develop the video and accompanying book in cooperation with its staff of experts and media analysts. Through the corporate partner, this product can be marketed to video rental chains to offer as a community service in their free-to-borrow section.

Steps to Safety. This kit includes a booklet of discount coupons on safety product guidelines for determining safe routes home from school, and a personal safety checklist to help avoid violent crime. Steps to Safety also features a packet with stickers children can affix in a booklet as they complete each lesson. Children can take the completed booklet to the corporate partner for free or discount-priced products.

The Conflict Resolution and Prevention Academy. This academy would be created with the help of a partner who shares a vested interest in decreasing crime in the community, such as an insurance company, local police department or university. The academy would provide classes and controlled experiences in conflict resolution and violence prevention at various levels of sophistication for African American children, teens and adults. Individuals and families could participate in the academy through videos, correspondence courses or classes in local community centers. Police and university representatives would be enlisted to help manage the academy. Academy training could become a prerequisite for future professional opportunities in law enforcement, social work and community leadership.

Idea 19

Organization: Private Financial Institution
Subject Area: Children – Financial Education
Keyword Search: youth, banking, customer loyalty, financial education, money, family finances

---

Strategy
Change the negative perceptions that youth in the market area have about this financial institution. Win young people over to the institution, and build long-term relationships with them that will encourage loyalty to the institution well into adulthood.

Underlying Value
Recognizing that success with the bottom line ultimately depends upon the community in which it is serving, the bank will build a business that cares about the young families and youth that are the future backbone of the institution. At the same time, it will earn the respect and admiration of the community, the loyalty of current customers and increased business that results from a positive reputation.

Components
It is never too early for kids to learn about money management and financial citizenship. This financial institution can play a key role in preparing young people to form socially responsible companies. This serves to establish its reputation as the financial institution that provides young people with the encouragement and tools they need to achieve successful, dual bottom lines. Using the resources already available within the institution, the bank can teach youth about responsible money management.

Execution
Youth Bank. This bank would be created as an extension of the financial institution's regular services. It would feature a separate lobby with lower counters to accommodate its shorter customers. It would offer the same full range of serv-

ices, such as checking and savings accounts, certificates of deposit, loans, credit cards, automated teller machine (ATM) cards and investment advice, but they would be tailored to the needs and experience of youth. Youth could buy stock in the company and even sit on a youth advisory board. The young board members would provide the bank with a youth's perspective. At the same time, they would gain insight into business practices (particularly those of financial institutions) and learn how an adult board of trustees operates.

Youth Trust. This not-for-profit foundation would provide educational programs for young customers, their parents and grandparents. The trust could fund a loan pool for young entrepreneurs. Traditional donations could fund educational programs such as a traveling interactive town, interactive games on the company's Web site and special camps or clubs.

Partners. The company could form a network of business customers or potential customers to be known as "Company X Business Partners." These companies could partner with the financial institution on various projects to support socially responsible youth enterprises. At the same time, they would be partnering with charitable organizations. These projects would enhance the organization's reputation for social responsibility, and may make it eligible for preferred interest rates on loans and other financial benefits. Charities that are supported by the company could be known as "Company X Community Partners."

Financial Competency, Conscience Management and Hands-on Learning. These concepts would all be taught in a "learn by doing" format. Regular weekend and evening classes would be offered to local families at the bank branch. Classes would cover subjects like:

- Kid's Money (allowance and personal financial management)
- On Time (credit management)
- Money Grows (effective saving and investing)
- Wise Buys, Caring Ties (careful spending and joyful giving)
- Better Futures (how to start and build a socially responsible business).

Another approach is to allow kids an opportunity to learn by playing the roles of banker, businessperson, mayor and so on, in an environment that simulates how the American economy works. The institution could make it available to all customers by means of a traveling exhibit. Or, the concept could be developed for computers, as either an interactive, online game or a computer game.

Savings Bonuses. To reinforce the lessons they learned from classes, the customers could join Youth Savings Club games and other activities sponsored by the Youth Trust. Savings club members would be eligible to receive "bonuses" for reaching certain savings milestones. Bonuses could take the form of discount merchandise vouchers or cash bonuses. For example, a $10 bonus could be added to the account for every $100 of new principal that is deposited and kept there for a minimum of sixty days. In addition, kids could receive a Caring Passport that is signed or stamped for every hour of volunteer service given to the company's Community Partners charity.

Youth Card. In addition to the ordinary ATM card, the company may consider offering a special Youth Card that would have both ATM and credit card capabilities. The card could be issued to young customers who maintain a Youth Bank Account for at least six months and meet certain criteria such as good grades, no drug use or police problems and completion of the On Time credit management class.

Idea 20

Organization: Child Care Provider and Learning Center
Subject Area: Children – Health Education
Keyword Search: children, teddy bear, free health clinic, health education, medical exam

---

Strategy

Position the child care center as the authority in preschool care by hosting a free "stuffed animal clinic," a system-wide program that serves several important needs for the center and the community.

Underlying Value

Stuffed animal clinics boost the center's audience with their entertaining, mediagenic events that attract many people.

- They give the center a chance to say to the community, "We are experts in early childhood care and education. We can help you be the best family you can be."
- They confirm the consumer's decision to send a child to the center. The

clinic sends the message: "We are more than just a day care center. We care about the overall health of your family."
- They help the organization serve the whole community by providing an enjoyable way for families to learn together about good health, household safety and visits to the doctor.
- They build alliances between the center and various businesses and organizations in the community that help develop the event.
- They create an opportunity for fun among center staff members. Preparing the clinic will give the staff a chance to develop and implement new ideas.

Components

The one-day Stuffed Animal Clinic can be held on a Saturday for a few hours. With help from community agencies, the center will become a "day animal clinic" with a number of health-related activity areas.

Height, Weight and Temperature. Part of a medical exam is having a patient's height, weight and temperature checked. This activity can help children feel comfortable with these procedures by letting them practice on their stuffed animals. Nursing students, volunteers or staff (all dressed in nurse uniforms) can help children administer these tests to their bears. Then, they can ask the children if they would like to have their own measurements taken.

Hearing Test or Screening and Podiatry Check. A local audiologist and a podiatrist can be invited to administer tests to check hearing and feet (and paws). Again, children can have their bears tested first then decide whether they would like to be tested as well.

Nutrition Center. A local nutritionist can be invited to teach children, animals and parents to make healthy, no-cook snacks with ingredients donated by a local supermarket. This activity can be supplemented with "Nutritional Discovery Games" and a display of rubber models of nutritious foods that may already be on hand at the center.

Bones. Most kids love bones and skeletons. Representatives from a hospital could bring a portable x-ray viewer and x-rays so kids would be able to see what real bones look like. The zoo or natural history museum might supply animal skeletons or x-rays.

Emergency Vehicles. Most fire and police departments will send their vehicles to community events subject to availability. This gives the kids a chance to climb on the fire truck and meet real firemen and policemen. If the local hospital has a Flight for Life helicopter, they could be invited to park it outside the center. Kids would love to watch it take off if it needed to respond to a call.

Handicapped Dolls. Dolls such as Shadow Buddies represent various physical disabilities, injuries and other conditions. A toy store or local child care center representative could bring them in and talk with children about disabilities. Kids would learn how a person can compensate for a disability. Other features might include a wheelchair kids can try, a maze the children can navigate while blindfolded and using a cane, a button hook, a communications board, and other equipment that will help kids understand disabilities through experiential play.

Stuffed Animal Triage. This role play doctor's office would be managed by volunteers and staff. Any equipment already available in the center could be used along with loaner items from a hospital or clinic. The staff and volunteer medical personnel could help kids listen to their heartbeat, take their blood pressure, pretend to give a shot to a stuffed animal, wrap a pretend wound, "set bones," try on uniforms, and learn about other common medical procedures. The kids should be allowed to practice on their stuffed animals first if they wish.

Fitness Center. The center could invite a children's gym to hold mini exercise classes at the clinic. The whole family can participate. Instructors could offer handouts describing exercises that family members can do together at home. The learning center may choose to create the fitness center from existing resources.

Parent Information Center. This quiet area would be staffed by medical specialists with whom parents can briefly discuss specific concerns. Ideally, this area would be adjacent to the Stuffed Animal Triage so children can play while their parents talk. Parenting magazines, such as *Parents* and *Working Mother*, could be made available for parents to read.

Celebrity Demonstrations. A local sports hero (from a professional, high school or college team) could demonstrate how to prevent and care for sports injuries.

The medical activities could be supplemented with a number of related activities, including the following.

Portraits. A commercial photographer could photograph children or families alongside a celebrity or a mascot for the center. They might also be photographed wearing a doctor's uniform or their personalized hospital gown, either engaged in a "medical activity" or striking a formal pose. Each family could receive a customized photo frame with the name and date of the event as well as the center's name and address printed on it.

Day Care. This standard center would allow children to drop in and look around. While the children play, one of the staff teachers can talk to parents about the center.

Information Area. This is the center's biggest chance to build enrollment since it will have a captive audience enjoying the center. An informational booth will allow staff to give out literature, answer questions and tell parents why this center is the best choice for their child. The center can also give away a toy (representative of the stuffed animal theme) to each family that enrolls a child.

Animal Cookie Center. The center could provide some animal cookie cutters and pre-made dough, so the kids can press out and decorate animal cookies. The cookies could be baked in the center's oven (if available) or a portable oven.

Book Display and Sale. A local bookstore could bring in adult and children's books on parenting, health and emotional issues. Bookstore staff should be available to discuss the books with parents.

Face Painting. Children love to paint their faces. The center could provide washable face paints or watercolors, along with mirrors and tissues, and let the kids enjoy themselves. Volunteers can supervise and provide suggestions.

Contests and Drawings. Throughout the event, the center could hold contests for visitors, such as:

- Who can diaper a doll the fastest (maybe for child/father teams)
- Stuffed animal look-alike contest
- Smallest/biggest stuffed animal contest
- Oldest/newest stuffed animal contest.

Stuffed Animals and Friends. Many companies use bears as symbols. The center could invite them all to add to the festivities. Possibilities include Winnie the Pooh (Sears), Billy Bob (Show Biz Pizza), Bucky Bear (Village Inn), Smokey the Bear (The USDA Forest Service), Scrubby Bear (American Red Cross) and Buckle Bear (SafetyBeltUSA / Weiner-Seaman Productions). Advertising their presence ahead of time would attract families and media.

Execution

A stuffed animal clinic should always include the "three P's"–partners, premiums and promotion. Both businesses and nonprofits can partner with the center to stage the event by providing money, volunteers to staff it, activities, premium items to give away, publicity and credibility.

Partnerships can lead to productive associations after the event is over as well. Potential partners include:
- Medical, dental, and nursing schools
- Nonprofit and for-profit medical chains
- Nonprofit medical centers, such as a university hospital or clinic
- Children's health specialists
- Poison control centers
- High school work programs, such as HERO (Home Economics Related Occupation)
- Junior Nurses Association
- Physicians and therapists in private or group practice (such as pediatricians, family practitioners, dentists, podiatrists, nutritionists and audiologists)
- Toy stores (local or national)
- State or city health departments
- Local representatives or distributors of pharmaceutical manufacturers (children's vitamins, pain relievers and cold remedies)
- Realtors and home builders
- Insurance companies
- Banks
- Local representative of baby food or related products
- Department stores or children's clothing stores
- Bookstores
- Community colleges
- Supermarkets
- Family restaurants.

The partner's name should be included on any flyers, press releases or advertisements that are used to publicize the event.

Premiums, or give-away items offered during the event, should be small things families can use at home to remind them of the clinic. These items should come from corporate partners. Potential premiums include:
- Toy medical equipment from a local toy store

- Health-related stickers from a hospital or toy store
- Growth chart from a pediatrician, children's welfare agency, or the local distributor of infant formula or baby food
- Children's vitamins from a supermarket or local distributor
- Hospital ID bracelets from a hospital or hospital supply store (with the center's logo printed on them)
- First aid kits from the Red Cross or the local representative of a manufacturer such as Johnson and Johnson
- Emergency phone number stickers from the phone company, poison control center, police department or fire department
- Dental hygiene products (toothbrushes, floss and mouthwash) from local dentists or dental supply stores
- Activity books from community health and safety agencies (coloring or activity books that teach the agency's message)
- Free or "two for one" coupons from local family entertainment centers (museums, zoos, sports facilities, amusement parks)
- Certificate of health featuring the center's logo; children could receive them as they exit the event.

Promotion of the event will be dependent on media coverage. The center can start generating media interest in a number of ways:

- Place an ad in the local newspaper.
- Create flyers advertising the event.
- "Plant" a feature story in the newspaper by calling the features editor several weeks ahead of time and describing the event.
- Grab the attention of the feature editor at each newspaper, television and radio station by sending a tongue depressor with the name and date of the event printed on it. Include a one-page description of the event and who to contact for more information.
- Have corporate partners include the event in their own advertising.

Community

Idea 21

Organization: Nonprofit Crime Prevention Organization
Subject Area: Community – Crime Prevention
Keyword Search: crime prevention, telethon, home security, personal security, crime prevention, Neighborhood Watch, block clubs

Strategy
Increase the organization's profile by providing education, resources and tools on preventing crime in neighborhoods across the nation.

Underlying Value
Adjustments to the already established National Crime Prevention Week will provide an excellent way to introduce compelling information about the organization–including its products and services–to every household. This

initiative will revitalize National Crime Prevention Week while advancing the organization's mission.

Components

A national fundraising telethon would provide corporate marketing partners with the opportunity to announce their relationship with the organization. Products and services co-produced with the organization would be featured, always promoting the brand name.

Through a national teleconference that links thousands of people via telecommunications, the organization would send the message that even when they are not face to face, people can collaborate to make progress toward a safer society. Hosting this practical discussion during National Crime Prevention Week is an excellent way to rally the public in its commitment to the cause.

A third leg of this initiative would be a traveling exhibit that brings information to the people. A corporate partner or partners would co-create and distribute the exhibit.

Execution

National Fundraising Telethon. This event would feature videos of local heroes and Neighborhood Watch success stories. Celebrities would not only entertain, but also make public commitments to help the organization in its crusade for safer communities. The telethon would offer opportunities for the public to make cash contributions, but also to sign up for local workshops or join a Neighborhood Watch.

The benefits that the organization provides to its members would be mentioned regularly, with telephone operators available to fill out membership applications (and add callers to the database). Telethon hosts would constantly remind viewers that by participating in the organization's programs, they can indeed help prevent crime.

National Teleconference. Corporate marketing partners and their employees would participate, along with schools where related programs have been introduced. Local clubs and organizations, as well as social groups (reached through neighborhood meeting places) would also be invited to help. Their dialogue with the organization and its spokespersons would focus on what has been happening and what still needs to be done. This gives the organization an opportunity to promote new programs and marketing partnerships, and report on recent successes.

Traveling Exhibits. In honor of National Crime Prevention Week, the organization would produce displays for public buildings such as airports, train stations and libraries. These would exhibit security devices for homes, businesses and public places and provide take-away information about the organization. It would publicize membership and volunteer opportunities as well. Interactive exhibits would allow visitors to experiment with crime prevention technology, such as personal safety alarms, locks and security lighting.

These exhibits would travel throughout the year but would be placed in highly concentrated population centers during National Crime Prevention Week.

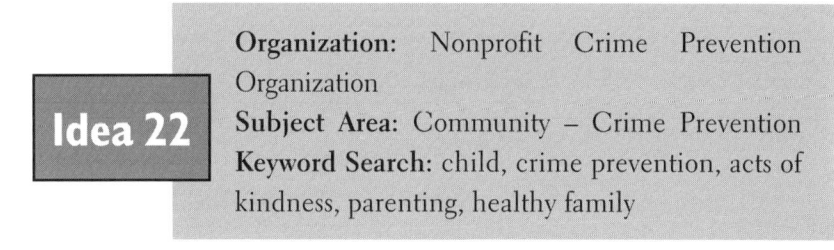

Idea 22

Organization: Nonprofit Crime Prevention Organization
Subject Area: Community – Crime Prevention
Keyword Search: child, crime prevention, acts of kindness, parenting, healthy family

---

Strategy
Establish a strong brand name that represents the organization's mission to reduce and prevent crime in order to create safer communities.

Underlying Value
Several childhood factors have been consistently and significantly linked to later teenage offending, including poor parental supervision; harsh, neglectful or erratic discipline; and parental discord. As a national advocate for families, this organization would have the opportunity to shift further from reactive to proactive strategies for preventing crime. It would shift to offering products directed at reducing poverty, ignorance and neglect, thereby helping prevent the circumstances that lead to criminal behavior.

Components
The organization would narrow the products and services it offers to three main thematic areas: families, youth and neighborhoods. Although these themes share

different initiatives, they all share a common goal–to equip constituencies to meet the challenges of creating safer communities. The organization would gain revenue and benefit from the increased traffic.

Execution

No More Victims Kit. These materials–puppets, music tapes, books and posters–help children and their parents change attitudes that contribute to violence. Each teaches a set of skills: how not to be a victim and how to manage impulsive and aggressive behavior. Families also learn both sides of the victimization issue: perpetrating violence and being subject to it. Children would be encouraged to explore problems and feelings, to solve problems and get along with others.

Issues such as gang involvement, bullying and peer pressure could be covered. Producers of educational materials for schools and schools themselves, but also booksellers, department stores and family magazines make excellent primary partners with the organization. The kit could be offered as a subscription renewal premium.

Child Protection Program. In cooperation with a video store or retailer of video cameras and videocassette recorders (VCRs), the organization could coordinate a child ID system. A short video would be made of the child to document his or her appearance and mannerisms. In addition, fingerprinting and labels for clothing would be offered to improve a parent's plan for dealing with a lost or abducted child. Parents could opt to "purchase" the video, fingerprints and clothing labels with a donation to the organization.

Caring Coupons. Here is a way to build self-esteem among all family members. The organization coupon booklets would be issued free to children from kindergarten to sixth grade. The children would then present individual coupons to a parent or other adult as a reward system for good behavior. Local businesses would agree to redeem these coupons at their outlets. For example, coupons could offer a free drink with a purchase at McDonald's or discounts on movie tickets and seats at cultural events.

These participating companies (the organization's marketing partners) would pay the organization for the right to market the coupons. The company would generate new sales while championing caring relationships and the value of a child.

Idea 23

Organization: Youth Crime Prevention Organization
Subject Area: Community – Crime Prevention
Keyword Search: youth, crime prevention, summer job fair, insurance policy, education

Strategy
Establish a strong brand name that represents the organization's mission to reduce and prevent crime in order to create safer communities.

Underlying Value
Youth are the future. Without the security of a happy and peaceful future, what investment will they make? This initiative focuses on youth for this simple reason. Through education and opportunity, two goals are achieved: the short-term reduction of criminal behavior and the long-term building of a climate of hope for tomorrow's leaders.

Components
The organization will narrow the products and services that it offers to three main thematic areas: families, youth and neighborhoods. Although these themes drive different initiatives, they share the common goal of equipping people to meet the challenges of creating safer communities.

Execution
Youth Insurance Policy. At modest rates, pre-teens and teens would purchase insurance for their personal belongings, including bicycles. This gives youth the perception of the rights and worth assigned to adult personal property. To teach responsibility, the insurance would cover vandalism or theft, but not loss that arises from neglect. The policy stresses the youth's role as a partner in crime prevention. Bicycle, rollerblade and skateboard manufacturers are all potential corporate partners, along with insurance companies. A percentage of the profits would go to the organization.

Summer Opportunity Fair. Youth need two kinds of work information: where they can get a job and what training they need to qualify for a job. Companies need an expedient way to interview young candidates for jobs as well as a forum for recruiting young people with good potential. The organization could rent space to companies at such a fair, with discounts if the company secures a booth at different fairs throughout the region. Young people might pay a small fee for admission to the fair, but only if they have assurances that genuine opportunities will likely result from their investment. Sales of advertising in the fair's program booklet, sales of Organization X products from booths, and sales of individual memberships could also generate profits.

Passport to Education. Youth often see little tangible benefit from doing well in school. In this passport, teachers would apply stamps indicating good grades, improved behavior or initiative towards a career goal. The fastest way to accumulate passport stamps would be to actively participate in an Organization X program. The passport would provide advertising space for youth product manufacturers and retailers to encourage youth to do well in school. These corporate partners would also announce discounts on purchases when a certain number of passport stamps are accumulated. A bank might even offer cash to students, with the stipulation that the youth directly deposit the money into a savings account at that facility and leave it for at least six months. Students would receive incentives that are truly motivating and businesses would get new customers.

Idea 24

Organization: Youth Crime Prevention Organization
Subject Area: Community – Crime Prevention
Keyword Search: crime, crime reduction, Neighborhood Watch, service projects, citizen police academy

Strategy
Establish a strong brand name that represents the organization's mission to reduce and prevent crime in order to create safer communities.

Underlying Value
There is a great power in pride. Personal pride builds self-esteem; family pride diminishes abuse; and neighborhood pride preserves a genuine sense of

community. Pride is evident in a healthy community; it can be seen in the renovation of a vandalized property or an increase in neighborhood safety because children have been educated to make wiser choices. This strategy capitalizes on and promotes community pride, and thus positions the organization as a proactive agent for social change rather than a reactive resource when crime hits close to home.

Components

The organization will narrow the products and services that it offers to three main thematic areas: families, youth and neighborhoods. Although these themes drive different initiatives, they share the common goal of equipping people to meet the challenges of creating safer communities. The organization will spearhead the efforts of neighbors, houses of worship, businesses and other nonprofits to revitalize neighborhoods throughout the region. It can also publicize the reclamation of streets that were once lost to crime and violence.

Execution

Welcome to the Neighborhood. This box or basket would include sample products from local retailers, information on schools, public transportation and community services, and coupons for household products. It would also include an application for membership in the organization as well as the organization's family safety information. Real estate agents would purchase the box or basket for their clients. The organization's corporate partners would pay to be included in the welcome kit. Proceeds would go directly to the organization and its programs in the cities where the product is sold.

Neighborhood Service Pack. This set of cards functions like a free catalog that includes removable coupons. Corporate partners would participate to encourage volunteer service to the consumer's neighborhood. Each coupon would list service projects that are coordinated by the organization such as tree plantings, neighborhood safety workshops or graffiti removal. They would also announce that participation in a service project will bring discounts on corporate partners' products and services.

Banks could also participate in the venture. The bank would make a donation to its existing or future customers for service performed in the community. The organization gets increased participation and motivated customers for its branded products. Corporate partners get new business.

The Citizen Police Academy. This partnership between the organization, its local crime prevention affiliates and police departments allows citizens to learn about how police make decisions. Officers would be provided to teach participants about the process, including the underlying reasons and stresses involved in various decision. Participants would be chosen through nominations by the crime prevention group.

The academy would exist to increase the number of people in the community who work positively with the police. This would serve as an excellent training opportunity for anyone pursuing a career in criminal justice. The dialog between citizens and police is the most important benefit of the program, but the organization would directly benefit from the sale of publications, and audio and video recordings that summarize the academy's recommendations.

Idea 25

Organization: Private Advertising Agency
Subject Area: Community – Crime Prevention
Keyword Search: advertising agency, youth awards programs, character developmen

---

Strategy
Position the agency as a corporation and a brand with a reputation for genuineness and passionate social responsibility.

Underlying Value
The agency can become a business characterized as much by its passion for social good as its passion for creative and financial success. This strategy will communicate a "Vision with Values Guarantee."

Components
The agency will promote the message: "Nothing should stop us–not even a lack of time or energy–from caring for others. We must care because the need is so great and our resources are so plentiful." In order to encourage younger generations in socially responsible behavior and revitalize compassionate action, the agency will publicize the good deeds of average citizens. It can

also sell products through the convenience of catalog shopping to raise funds for important projects.

Execution
Award Programs. The agency could sponsor (and individual clients could co-sponsor) a series of awards honoring those who make a difference. The awards would be publicized through print advertising. The agency would set up a "Charitable Services Fund" to pay for these initiatives. The ads would generate public support and draw the attention of potential clients who want to be aligned with a high profile charity. Awards would include:

- The Angels in Action Award – national search to find someone who responded well to a crisis, an angel who was ready to help
- The Giraffe Project – a project that seeks out and honors those who have been willing to stick their necks out for the common good (an idea that continues to garner publicity)
- The Children's Challenge – an award for boys and girls who have made a difference in their community.

Create-a-Card Kiosks. In partnership with a greeting card and/or computer company, the agency would sponsor these touch sensitive screens that would be set up in public places. The agency's creative staff would produce a set of images related to caring for others, with appropriate messages such as "You have made a difference in my life" or "Thanks for being there." This product offers customers an easy way to express caring for someone they know as well as people they do not know. The kiosk would advertise the purchase of the personalized greeting that includes a donation to one of the agency's charitable causes.

Idea 26

Organization: Crime Prevention Organization
Subject Area: Community – Crime Prevention
Keyword Search: crime prevention, safety kit, auto theft prevention, bike lock

Strategy
Strengthen the reputation of the organization as the nation's number one crime fighter and resource for crime prevention education.

Underlying Value

The organization can use marketing projects to carry its message to the public. These projects, unlike creating and maintaining new programs, are moneymakers. Each of them should cover its cost in addition to generating a profit.

Components

Targeted corporations can be invited to market products associated with the strategy. Potential partners include small and large businesses, national and local organizations (scouts, Jaycees and other community organizations), and social service agencies, among others. In addition to receiving benefits and premiums for their customers and employees, they will want to use this organization as a means to their own service ends.

Execution

Safety Snoop Kit. This kit would be offered as part of a catalog membership benefit or as a stand-alone premium item for corporate buy-ins. The kit would include the organization's mascot "Safety Snoop Badge," discount coupons, a catalog with safety products, a home safety checklist in the form of a game, and possibly a "safe route to school" game. A safety sticker book would also be included. Family members would fill in the stickers each time a child completes a safety step. The "Safety Snoop Kit" is ideal for interactive membership. Once the "Safety Audit Sticker Book" is completed, the family could send it to the organization. The organization would send it back with an official "Safety Snoop Card" and window decal certifying that the house is protected by the organization's mascot, and thus, by the organization. Upon receiving their card, family members would be enrolled in a sweepstakes. Cards would be drawn at random, and the winning family would receive a trip to Disneyland or another family vacation spot.

A free membership or membership discount would serve as a premium. A corporate partner could invest in the program by providing kit underwriting, kit production and fulfillment of the premiums.

Auto Theft Prevention Kit. This kit would be offered for pre-sell to car dealers and manufacturers as well as to automotive clubs. It would include a list of theft prevention tips, a safety window decal, discount coupons for auto alarms, and a branded litter bag.

Bike Out of Crime. Through this partnership with a bike lock company or bike manufacturer, bikers would receive a branded decal and bike safety kit when they present proof of bike registration. It would be managed on a local level by volunteers, members or staff. It could be offered during "National Bike Safety Week." As part of the promotion, the organization could host bike safety seminars, bike repair mini-classes, and demonstrations of both fancy bike riding and safe biking habits. The main focus should be safety and crime prevention through bike registration.

The organization could also launch a national promotion that is coordinated with the National Bike Registry and a local bike manufacturer: The organization would receive one dollar each time the manufacturer's bike lock is purchased. Cents-off coupons would be distributed through the local bike registry office for discounts on bike locks.

Idea 27

Organization: National Trust for the Preservation of Heritage
Subject Area: Community – Culture and Heritage
Keyword Search: heritage, culture, books, postcards, cookbooks, family tree

Strategy

Become a nationally recognized and celebrated definer of personal history and creator of heritage opportunities for businesses, community groups and the general public. Measurable terms and goals include:
- Earned income will double the amount of lottery money the trust has available to give away.
- The number of corporations involved in heritage projects will double each year.
- The public's results on a "heritage quiz" will improve fifty percent over six years.

Underlying Value

Most heritage products engage the users–child or adult history buffs–in a discovery process, helping them connect with and feel their heritage. They celebrate intangibles such as nostalgia, regional pride and ethnic pride. The organization can create a product line that represents the best of these.

Merchandise would include books, kits and paper products that can generate considerable income for the trust. All of the products would celebrate and popularize heritage at a human and intensely personal level. They would celebrate the fact that history is right where a person lives, and that it includes every thing in a person's surroundings.

Components

Brag Book. This book for homeowners would show the before, during and after phase of the building or renovations of their home. Real estate companies may be interested in these for their customers who purchase homes. It could also be available from building supply stores throughout the country when the customer purchases a specific product.

Postcard Book. This book of detachable postcards would depict fascinating historic sites. Membership in a heritage society could be offered as a premium. An automobile association may want to offer a membership, too. The book would carry the message: "Wish you were here and there and there...."

Cook-Look Books. These books celebrate regional and ethnic cuisine. They take the reader into the homes of Native Americans and those whose heritage is Irish, Jewish, Swedish, Japanese or any other nationality. The recipes, photographs and interviews with the family or individual showing their homes entice the reader to eat his or her way through a mosaic of cultures. This partnership opportunity is ideal for a food company.

Village Street Scenes. Charming, mini-cardboard constructions of scenes and sites that are historically rich would feature traditional homes, houses of worship, commercial and government buildings and other structures that are native to the region.

"Baseball" Cards. This set of cards would feature pictures and details about the lives of famous historical figures. Convenience stores could promote the cards in their outlets throughout the year on an exclusive basis. The cards would feature both living and deceased people, their date and place of birth, interests, career and personal highlights. Notable deeds would also be included. Individual cards or a complete set could become valuable collectibles when the

Family Time Capsule. The capsule encourages family members to preserve items that mark their unique place in time. The kit would include suggestions on using it for births, graduations, marriages and other memorable occasions.

Replicas. These miniatures would depict distinctive, nationally important houses and cottages, and villages, town sites and heritage sites. They would be chosen based on distinctive architecture and could include homes, corporate offices, classic structures and new buildings with unique design.

Executive Reproductions. These "limited edition replicas" would include reproductions of desks, lamps, paperweights, blotters, inkwells, prints, stained glass and other items from the offices of historic homes. They could also be sold through high-end furniture stores.

Execution

Heritage Hamlets. These upscale mini-stores would sell the trust's products and services, including the books, kits and other products mentioned above. They would also sell high quality artisan works and other items that were produced in that region or country. They avoid the current glut of catalog promotions but build on the interest in such products that the catalogs create. The trust receives a percentage of all sales.

The hamlets would be housed in high traffic areas like malls, shopping districts and historic areas of town. A high tech variation would feature a computer terminal where consumers can order items online.

All variations allow the trust to control production, pricing and promotion of its products. Local "living legends" or celebrated artisans could be on hand for the grand opening of each hamlet. The hamlets could be centers for cross promoting a number of heritage-related events such as movie and book releases, notable anniversary dates and so on.

Idea 28

Organization: National Trust for Heritage Preservation
Subject Area: Community – Culture and Heritage
Keyword Search: preservation, historic, neighborhood, family heritage

Strategy

Become a nationally recognized and celebrated definer of personal history and creator of heritage opportunities for businesses, community groups and the general public. Measurable terms and goals include:

- Earned income will double the amount of lottery money the trust has to give away
- The number of corporations involved in heritage projects will double each year.
- The average citizen's results on a "heritage quiz" will improve fifty percent over six years.

Underlying Value

By creating initiatives that popularize heritage, the trust will reinforce its mission while setting standards for organizing earned income events. These events are intended to introduce large numbers of new people to the trust and broaden its base significantly. If they successfully reflect the public's perception of what heritage is or might be, they will reinforce benefit the trust and its corporate partners.

Components

The organization will reach and educate the general public through exciting, highly visible promotions. Corporate sponsors can underwrite these promotions so that production costs are covered and a net profit remains for the trust. The corporate partners will look for measurable benefits that improve their competitive advantage in areas such as traffic building, deepened customer loyalty and selling higher margin merchandise.

Execution

Preservation Wagon Train. This one-time-only, blockbuster program would make history as it recreates it. The train would follow the original "gold rush" trail during a designated time of the year with a celebration at each stop. Exposure would be high for all concerned, as each step of the journey would be followed in the media.

A multitude of special events can be tied in with the wagon train. Each stop could be a meeting ground for community pioneers over age eighty. Or, each could showcase "living legends" from the area or region depending on which individuals have more public appeal. Because of the media attention, residents would eagerly await the arrival of the wagon train in each town. Early evening "yarn spinning" would have communities enthralled as they sit by the campfire connecting with their past.

This promotion offers corporations an opportunity to buy and live a piece of history. Several corporations can sponsor an event of this magnitude. Some may wish to sponsor their employees to ride a portion of the trail. Others may choose to sponsor a part of it, such as a frontier reunion, community pioneers, or travel demonstrations by a legend. Local corporations can also choose these since the cost would be lower.

The trust would simply serve as a packager of the wagon train. The train itself would become a vehicle for a number of individuals and groups, both commercial and nonprofit, to celebrate town pride and focus attention on the wealth and importance of the area's physical and cultural heritage.

Historic Neighborhood Award. This national award would honor the bonds and elements that keep a neighborhood together over time. It would recognize neighborhoods that do not forget their past or present. The competition could start on a local level and result in a national designation for neighborhoods that expresses the elements (defined by the trust) which make a neighborhood great. These elements might include:

- Is characterized by interactive design
- Encourages community involvement
- Addresses the needs of the community (families, the elderly, or various ethnic groups)
- Has maintained a level of community pride and interaction for an easily tracked period of time
- Demonstrates a commitment to preserve and promote its cultural and architectural heritage.

Awards can be based on types and sizes of communities, such as urban and rural, established and newly developed, located in large and small cities, and so on. Entries could be made via photographs, drawings, videos, or other visuals with appropriate narratives that address the criteria established by the trust.

The contest should be structured to encourage community members to form "teams." These groups would review their neighborhoods, investigate neighborhood elements that meet the contest criteria, and prepare the visuals and narratives.

Idea 29

Organization: Organization for Educational Awareness of Black Americans in Western United States
Subject Area: Community – Culture and Heritage
Keyword Search: traveling exhibit, hero, public schools, Black American, African American, heritage, cultural awareness

Strategy

Re-establish the organization's identity to communicate its basic purpose and create an umbrella under which all of its programs fall. Rather than being a museum of artifacts of African Americans in the West, the organization would be a repository and promoter of pride in African American accomplishments–past, present and future.

Underlying Value

Thinking of the organization in the defined strategy opens up a wealth of program options that would not be available to a more narrowly defined museum. This positions the organization as a repository for history and a catalyst for social change.

Components

Four initiatives can be linked together to build momentum. They include programs, development, marketing and product development, and special events.

Execution

Traveling Exhibit. This portable, traveling exhibit would be developed with the use of artifacts from the organization's museum collection. In addition to carrying the organization's message out to the community, it would generate revenue. Developed with a grant from a corporation, it could be rented to schools, shopping centers and community centers to promote interest in and visibility for the organization.

Public School Solicitation. The organization can encourage interest among children in the neighborhood elementary schools by inviting them to complete the organization's branded puzzle of the museum (which happens to be in a house). Each room would constitute a puzzle piece. The students would begin with the puzzle dismantled. For every dollar the class contributes, they could add a room to the puzzle. When they complete the puzzle, they can put their class photo (or other personal decoration) on it and turn it in with their donation (approximately ten dollars total) to the organization.

The completed puzzles would go on display in the organization's museum so the children can see their picture exhibited. Churches and social clubs could also be targeted for participation.

Black Map of the City. The organization can create a map to educate the community about contributions that black business owners and real estate developers made to the city's (or region's) economy and landscape in the early days. This annotated and highly graphic map would show the African American presence in the city around the turn of the 20th Century. Land, buildings and businesses owned by African Americans would be shaded in different colors. The margins would be filled with facts and statistics about African Americans, both today and in the past, also shaded in different colors. A strong incentive to African American pride, the map could be offered to both a corporation as a premium item and to the organization's museum as merchandise.

Heroes. The organization can host a series of workshops for the general public. A prominent or popular African American person would lead each workshop. If the workshop concept does not appeal to a specific celebrity, the museum can hold lectures in large group settings and discussions in small group settings. As the event would be a fund-raiser, the celebrities would waive their regular fees for speaking engagements. Proceeds from ticket sales would go to the organization.

Idea 30

Organization: Private Consumer Goods Company
Subject Area: Community – Culture and Heritage
Keyword Search: culture, sacred sites, architecture, paintings, sculpture, heritage, cultural awareness

Strategy

Establish a marketing program that supports the company's business agenda and makes a positive difference for the culture and heritage society.

Underlying Value

The company will be known as a champion of living celebrations of the past, present and future as well as appreciation for the natural world and the human family. It will also be known for encouraging those aspects of society that transform mere existence into an exuberant experience of life.

Components

One way to achieve the stated strategy is through the Historic Preservation Initiative. The products and signature events will help residents to celebrate their past and value their ethnic, social and even architectural heritage.

Execution

Sacred Sites Tiles. Whether for use as trivets or simply for display, this set of ceramic tiles would celebrate cherished locations throughout the country. With each purchase of these tiles, the company would make a donation to groups that are preserving these and other important historic places. The marketing literature would encourage the purchaser to collect the tiles and offer ideas for display or practical uses.

Limited Editions. Through retail displays and in print advertising, the company would promote the sale of commissioned works of arts. The paintings, sculptures and reproductions would benefit like-minded partners who share the mission of preserving heritage. The product would be available only to customers who present ten of the company's product labels. The product itself could promote sale of the art, while the limited edition images would be echoed on product labels.

A Regional or National Day. This all-day summer street party would take place simultaneously in cities nationwide, culminating in the company-sponsored fireworks display. It would encourage people to get out and enjoy historic parks for holiday picnics. Coupons for the company's products would be sold with a special hook: Because this company believes in celebrating the regional or national heritage, on Region X Day, proceeds from sales of specific brands will go to civics education projects or historical museums.

Local organizations, such as a chamber of commerce or tourism council, would likely cooperate with the organization on these events, providing marketing and advertising support as well as logistical information for planning purposes.

Idea 31

Organization: National Professional Trade Association for Architecture
Subject Area: Community – Culture and Heritage
Keyword Search: architecture, heritage, buildings, historical landmarks

Strategy

Develop a long-term strategy with various levels of activity, based on three goals. First, capitalize on the association's current expertise, resources and strengths. Second, build on those as well as the organization's purposes. And third, reflect the organization's fundamental goals of becoming more self-reliant and diversifying its revenue base.

Underlying Value

All levels of marketing will represent the following values:

- This organization is the leader in demystifying architecture by translating architectural standards to the public in lay terms.
- The organization exhibits and celebrates the qualities, skills and diversity of architects and architecture.
- The organization's foundation is placed in the center of all activity, so it can "test the future," establish a vision and introduce programs that excite the staff and public.

Components

The trade association would create products and promotions that garner the most attention from professionals in this field and from the organization's target audience. The organization should also increase and encourage individual risk-taking within the staff, reward clever and fresh ideas, and introduce an employee bonus system that rewards the service corporation for profitability and objectives accomplished under budget.

Execution

Paper Models of Famous Buildings. These easily constructed sets of familiar, famous buildings would be packaged to illustrate a type of construction or period of history. Packaged as collectors' items, they would be available in modern, historic, traditional and classical themes. Variations in plastic and/or wood could also be available for the high-end market.

Build-a-Home Board Game. This game could be structured in the style of a board game such as Monopoly or Trivial Pursuit, except it would be based on knowledge of structures, professional relationships and the building process. The object of the game would be to build a home in an entertaining, educational and creative way. The main target audience would be the Baby Boomer market. The game makes an excellent premium item for the real estate industry.

Pop-up Book Series. This entertaining series of pop-up publications would demonstrate the three-dimensional nature of architecture as well as the creativity and imagination that architects employ in their work. The series can be made available to various market bands: the general public, the collector or connoisseur, and the professional. The tremendous variety of disciplines and outstanding examples of architecture can be celebrated. Book topics could include:
- Award winning art, architecture and landscape design
- Interior design
- Topical subjects
- Housing styles
- Architectural types and innovations
- Environmentally responsible design
- Historical landmarks
- The Statue of Liberty
- The Cathedral of Notre Dame
- The Pentagon
- The Taj Mahal
- The Eiffel Tower
- The Leaning Tower of Pisa.

The Great Brand X Toy Challenge. This national contest would be sponsored by a major building set manufacturer. The challenge would start on a local or regional level, progress to the state championships and conclude at the national or international level. The challenge would be to build a dream building, city, community, or other architectural wonder, using only the materials provided by the manufacturer. Contestants would be challenged to solve certain design problems:

- The design encourages pedestrian activity and reduces auto traffic and pollution.
- The design is energy efficient.
- The design is economically efficient.
- The design encourages interaction between people and their environment.

This challenge celebrates architecture as child's play. It is a great marketing and image builder for the sponsoring company (toys are for adults, too!). In addition, it encourages interaction between the general public and the architecture community. The contest, open to the public as well as the professional, would be judged by the architectural gurus and giants in the field.

Architecture Rich Cities. This American Institute of Architects designation recognizes cities that preserve, promote and encourage fine design. Once a city has qualified as an AIA-designated design rich city, AIA would promote it through AIA-designed plaques, banners, a map of high design areas and so on. National firms that wish to align their image with quality and craftsmanship could buy the licensing rights to the city's image to promote their corporation or their products. AIA would receive a management fee and percentage of the city's licensing fees.

Quality of Life Partnerships. These partnerships between the association and various corporations would promote a "quality of life" theme. The association would negotiate a series of product endorsements that would enable the corporation to promote their product(s) as a high quality interaction of form and function with the organization.

- Car Manufacturer X – "We don't build cars, we design them"
- Bank Y – "Loans designed for your lifestyle"
- Architectural Firm Z – "We design for your future."

Idea 32

Organization: Affordable Housing Provider
Subject Area: Community – Housing
Keyword Search: youth employment, home improvement, do-it-yourself, construction, home inspection, low income housing

Strategy

Become a national model for housing-oriented nonprofits. This advocate of affordable, sensible housing would also be educating youth who are interested in the construction trade.

Underlying Value

Instead of doing all things for all people, the organization will do a few things very, very well. These things include:
- Remain a specialist in helping low-income people buy homes and avoid defaulting on their ownership
- Work at the neighborhood level while creating national impact
- Honor the organization's roots by building on its history of success in affordable housing and construction.

Components

These services and products would turn the nonprofit into two organizations: a recharged, focused nonprofit and an aggressive, for-profit subsidiary that enters the commercial marketplace systematically and quickly.

Execution

The organization could create a range of services to serve a handful of niche markets. The "Trustworthy Handyman of the Middle Class" services would include two categories.

Help for Do-It-Yourselfers. Despite the home improvement boom, many do-it-yourselfers do not have the skills or confidence needed to complete certain projects on their own. They may need advice on the projects they are capable of doing and help from an experienced plumber, electrician, or roofer on the "really big" ones. The organization can provide help to these middle income homeowners by selling them its expertise at competitive market rates.

"I Wish I Didn't Have To" Chores. Cleaning gutters, caulking windows, repainting a fence and raking leaves are among those onerous, preventative maintenance tasks that most homeowners wish someone else would do. The organization can be that "someone else." They can package the performance of these chores and sell them at wholesale. Corporations and organizations would pay to make them available to their employees, customers and members.

Handicap Retrofit Service. The organization could contract advocate organizations for individuals with disabilities or diseases such as cerebral palsy or multiple sclerosis. It would become the official provider of retrofit construction work for those individuals. Serving the handicapped housing retrofit market would become the organization's subspecialty.

Builders Overstock Warehouse. The organization could create a retail sales operation in a donated warehouse. It would sell doors, windows, bricks, siding, trim, paint and other materials that builders, manufacturers and retailers have donated because it is more efficient than restocking, moving, selling or storing them. For this operation to remain nontaxable, it will need to meet some of the following criteria. First, it must be run by volunteers. Second, the materials sold must be donations. And third, the hours of operation must be "irregular" (that is, not every day or every week but seasonal, or anytime there is a large enough inventory gathered). Creating a name that does not sound like an ongoing business, such as the "Giant Builders' Overstock Garage Sale" would also help.

A number of products could be sold to help the homeowner or the person who is looking to buy a home.

Buyers Home Inspection Booklet. This booklet tells potential home buyers what to look for in the house of their dreams. It tells them how to determine whether it is as good a buy as they think it is. The booklet would be pre-sold to banks, real estate companies and mortgage companies.

Kits for the Do-It-Yourselfer. Kits to build a variety of "home-enhancing" items would contain everything the amateur needs to complete the job, from instructions and diagrams to lumber, hardware and varnish. The kits could be produced in a number of ways. For example, organization members could create the materials and then sell them in bulk to national retailers. The organization could also sell the design to national retailers who then manufacture and sell the items and pay the organization a royalty. Possible kits include:

- Greenhouse or sun room
- Children's furniture
- Picnic furniture or patio furniture
- Home security
- Storage shed or garage
- Dog house
- Doll house
- Bird houses
- Window flower boxes
- Storage shed or garage
- Gazebo
- Fences
- Indoor shelving

Idea 33

Organization: Housing Service Provider to Low Income Individuals and Families
Subject Area: Community – Housing
Keyword Search: community housing, civic involvement, low income, poverty, employee volunteers

Strategy

Alleviate poverty and improve the quality of life for residents and neighborhoods. Develop, finance and operate affordable housing that is community-based and resident-focused.

Underlying Value

Neighborhoods are designed in a way that people silently drive into their garages and never see their neighbors. Yet, they want to care about others and have others care about them; they yearn for it. However, most people do not know how to create this sense of community. By providing consumers with practical tools for learning how to build a participatory neighborhood, the organization will encourage civic-mindedness among residents of the same building or street.

Components

The organization could develop activities that help to create a civic-minded community and provide consumers with practical tools for learning how to build a participatory neighborhood.

Execution

Customer Volunteer Days. This idea is fast becoming a staple for customer-minded corporations like the auto manufacturer Saturn. Through advertising and point-of-sale strategies in retail outlets, customers are invited to join company employees in volunteer activities. Employees could volunteer to paint the homes of the organization's disabled residents or build a playground at one of the organization's sites. Not only do customers enjoy helping out, but they also like the conversations they share over the course of the day. This enables isolated and often affluent Americans to learn about participating in a community. In addition, customers who volunteer could receive discount coupons for merchandise or services.

Values Growth Chart. Teaching your children how to participate in a community can be difficult. Parents may be acquainted with very few role models of neighborliness and caring for those less fortunate. If so, they look for products that help them instill these values. The chart would record the child's growth not only in physical height but also in character. Each time a child practices an act of civic-mindedness (volunteering, assisting someone in need, performing a "random act of kindness"), his or her growth in moral stature would be recorded.

This product can also provide parents with practical guidelines for remaining an important a part of their community. The guidelines would demonstrate that participation is not that difficult when it is broken down into easy, understandable behaviors and practices.

Family Service Vacations. In recent years, tourism has seen the invention of an entirely new kind of vacation. Many people want to have fun and relax but also do something of social value, like volunteering for a cause. Often, they want this for their children, too. A family service vacation could be the answer. The organization's corporate partner would offer customers the chance to vacation for a week or a long weekend at a resort near one of the organization's sites. In exchange for volunteering several hours each day, participants would earn discounts on products or access to premium services.

Idea 34

Organization: Housing Service Provider to Low Income Individuals and Families
Subject Area: Community – Housing
Keyword Search: community development, social enterprise, small business awards, healthy communities

Strategy

Encourage an enterprising community that helps individuals celebrate opportunity and ingenuity in themselves, their families and the businesses they support. Position the organization and its partner as the nationally recognized leaders in identifying enterprising young people

Underlying Value

People learn to improvise when things break down and there is not enough money for repairs. Many residents served by this organization have experienced this life lesson and can share it with neighbors. Together, they can celebrate creative solutions and turn ingenuity into opportunity. Already, this organization's residents have created many a small business out of their talent for fixing things.

Components

All of the initiatives would celebrate practicality and ingenuity. This would, in turn, bring out the enterprising qualities that are inherent in healthy communities.

Execution

The (Really) Small Business Award. We hear about awards for successful entrepreneurs who have grown a business from a two-man show to a multibillion dollar conglomerate. This award will celebrate ingenuity and enterprise on a much smaller scale. The (Really) Small Business Award would highlight someone like an organization resident who has transformed a talent for artistically covering graffiti into a mural-painting business. Stories like this help build confidence in others; they inspire us to share our abilities with the community. To enhance this idea, the service provider could invite targeted customer groups and employees should be invited to participate in choosing the award winners.

Youth Social Enterprise Recognition. From time to time, individuals apply entrepreneurial techniques to perform exceptional public service–projects that directly impact the community. Spirits marketer Chivas Regal has coined the term "extrapreneur" to describe such individuals. Through an award program or as a media campaign, this recognition initiative would celebrate young entrepreneurs who make positive, exceptional contributions to public service.

Enterprise Learning Opportunities. This opportunity starts with the residents of the organization who have been encouraged by their neighbors to turn a talent into a business. To generate income for the organization, this community-wide venture would be sponsored by a corporate partner. Participants would learn how to produce a product that is valuable to the corporate partner's customers. They would also learn to market it with the message that each purchase supports the organization's communities.

The Organization X Smart Card. Like a frequent flyer membership, this card would get consumers involved in supporting the organization by signing them up to earn specific benefits. It could serve as a loyalty card as well as a credit card for making purchases. A unique feature allows consumers, when they redeem their benefits, to allocate some of that credit to the organization. Credit could take the form of cash or be specific products that a consumer has earned, such as tools or cleaning supplies that would be helpful to the organization's residents. As the residents succeed financially and move to permanent homes, the smart card would give them an opportunity to "give back" to the organization in a tangible way.

Idea 35

Organization: Housing Service Provider to Low Income Individuals and Families
Subject Area: Community – Housing
Keyword Search: friendly communities, healthy communities, shared community experience, neighborhoods

Strategy
Foster a friendly community that recognizes a desire among residents of all incomes to live in a familiar, secure environment where people share mutual concerns.

Underlying Value
A regular activity of this organization's residents is sharing food at potluck suppers, pancake breakfasts and holiday barbecues. Cultures across time and place have always known that one of the best ways to build community is to eat with one's neighbor. This is the kind of friendly exchange that is missing for hundreds of thousands of people, many of whom live in affluent suburbs and feel completely alone amidst acres of tract homes.

Components
The events and products listed below help consumers get ideas for building friendly communities. They also offer consumers the opportunity to make a difference for the organization's programs.

Execution

Community Barbecues. This monthly barbecue would be held at the local home products retail store. These "superstores" usually have rather large parking lots. Families would be encouraged to bring others; they would receive discounts for bringing neighbors. The proceeds from the barbecue could pay to install barbecue grills and picnic tables in the common areas of the organization's properties. The corporate partner benefits by being able to announce, "We bring communities together."

Comfort Food Contest. Several popular cookbooks on the market feature only non-gourmet recipes. From mashed potatoes to cream chipped beef on toast, old-time food favorites are becoming remarkably popular. This local contest would promote a search for the best comfort food. Folks "next door" would be invited to come taste their neighbors' great macaroni and cheese. A citywide comfort food cookbook would instill community pride and provide a great product for the average cook. Profits would go to the organization. Also, manufacturers and retailers of commercial foods could be enlisted as partners to dedicate a percentage of their sales to the organization.

Security Blankets. What friendly communities really bring us is a sense of security. We sleep better at night when we know our neighbors keep an eye out for us. This traditional product, the old stand-by baby blanket, would be marketed with several twists. First, it directly addresses the insecurity a small child feels when the blanket must be laundered. A smaller version of the blanket is tucked into a pouch at the corner of the larger one to provide security until the dry cycle is complete. Second, consumers would have a three-fold reason to buy. It makes a great gift for a friend or family member. Also, a portion of each purchase goes to the organization, where people watch out for one another and can get a hug when times are tough. Finally, the cost of the blanket is discounted if a second security blanket is purchased for a neighbor's child.

Adult Friendship Kits. It may seem simplistic, but many consumers need very basic instructions on how to be a friend. These branded kits include greeting cards for common occasions, holiday recipes designed to be shared, and suggestions for getting to know one's neighbor. Each kit purchased brings a donation to the organization. A "National Search for the Best Friend" promotion could accompany this product. Customers and employees would compete to define the personal characteristics people look for in others and hope to cultivate in themselves.

Children's Friendship Kits. A young person's version of the Adult Friendship Kit would include strings to make friendship bracelets, coloring books and pens that feature friends at play and an audio recording of songs about how to be a friend.

> **Idea 36**
>
> **Organization:** Affordable Housing Provider
> **Subject Area:** Community – Housing
> **Keyword Search:** friendly communities, healthy communities, shared community experience, neighborhoods

Strategy

Create clearly defined initiatives that position the provider as a valuable resource to business by establishing powerful links between its services and corporate partners who have products and services to market.

Underlying Value

Creating this membership program does not require significant investment of money, people or time. It positions the corporate partner as a valuable resource to a wide variety of businesses and corporations as well as to the public.

Components

The organization would develop and manage the "Healthy Communities Membership" program. It would be marketed primarily as a self-serving purchase opportunity and would be promoted through print advertising, promotional materials at home shows and real estate guides. After modest administrative costs are covered, the income from membership fees would go to funding the organization's programs.

Execution

Individual Membership. Individuals who purchase the membership will receive a quarterly newsletter that includes stories and tips for creating community in their own neighborhoods; cost effective ideas for retaining or enhancing the value of their homes; and empowerment education for kids. The newsletter will also include discount coupons for a variety of household products and services. Every application will advertise that cashing in even a portion of the newsletter coupons will pay for the cost of the membership. Coupons could include manufacturers' or retailers' discounts on building materials, efficient appliances, tools or replacement parts. National "superstore" retailers and local hardware and appliance chains make excellent coupon providers. Various public relations opportunities are available for local retailers or real estate agencies. For a fee, they can choose to sponsor the newsletter. This name recognition carries a lot of weight in a highly competitive market.

Business Membership. Organization X Coalition corporate members would see two major benefits. First, they would be positioned as a caring company, part of a team working to meet the housing needs of their low-income neighbors. Second, they would be buying recognition in the corporation's annual report and in advertising and public relations materials distributed via the *Healthy Communities Newsletter.*

An entry level business membership would include Healthy Communities benefits for both employees and customers, plus the opportunity to work with the organization to design promotions for future newsletters. A manufacturing company could introduce a new light and motion sensor or other neighborhood safety product to Healthy Communities members. The organization would help design the product promotion. For a modest investment, the company gains a unique avenue for providing incentives to purchase a new product and positive public relations for itself.

Local banks could market their home equity loan services to Healthy Communities members. They could offer individual members a great rate on a certificate of deposit or home equity loan while pledging a percentage of the profits to the organization's programs.

Idea 37

Organization: Public Radio and Television Station
Subject Area: Community – Recreation
Keyword Search: radio station, listener, music, service, reward, incentives

Strategy

Enhance the radio station's relationship with the listener by creating interactive programs and new educational opportunities.

Underlying Value

To create a greater sense of ownership among its constituents, the station can promote the idea that it provides viewers and listeners with a valuable, responsive service that is prepared for the exciting opportunities of the future.

Components

Three components support this strategy. "Lifelong Learning" with the station offers customers a number of opportunities to act on their belief that education is important and learning should last a lifetime. "Civic Certification" provides people an opportunity to put practical skills to use to meet the needs of their community. "Service Currency" gives the station a means of touching the lives of its constituents by rewarding "obedience to the unenforceable."

Execution

Lifelong Learning with the Station. Citizens who sign on to the Lifelong Learning program could participate in electronic town square meetings with notable public servants. They could also sit on citizen panels to debate important issues or cases. This positions the station as an important educator, bridging the gap between the "information rich" and the "information poor."

Customers would pay a small premium for access to Lifelong Learning information. When they use this digital access, they know that a percentage of their purchase price–an annual subscription or a monthly fee–would go to help those who cannot pay the cost of a program that reduces the digital divide.

Civic Certification. This program would link customers with local opportunities, providing telephone numbers, class schedules and meeting locations to get involved in community affairs. It would also offer access to skills such as cardio-pulmonary resuscitation (CPR), the Heimlich Maneuver and other first aid; how to start a Neighborhood Watch or playground clean-up program; how to make a difference in local politics; and how to tutor or mentor disadvantaged children. Eventually, Civic Certification could become the average citizen's equivalent of earning the Eagle Scout distinction. It would recognize years of community service and the acquisition of skills that are useful to the community.

Participants would earn credits toward certain rewards through a "benefits package." The greater the community need and the more time people spend volunteering, the greater their rewards. All of these benefits would have social value, allowing individuals to feel that the station is concerned about their lives. For example, a certain number of Civic Certification credits would earn the donation of a computer to a local school.

Service Currency. This initiative allows citizens to earn the station's Service Currency when they use their resources to help others. By providing child or elder care, transportation, meals for a shut-in, home improvements or other services, the consumer can convert personal time into purchasing power. The currency would buy benefits for individuals or their family members. Another benefit it could buy would be membership in a club that gives the participant discounts on valued services.

The station would supply opportunities to earn Service Currency in their local communities. Also, people could combine their Service Currency to pay for the program to decrease the digital divide for a low-income family.

This reward system would also apply to "random acts of kindness." Citizens or their admirers could report the good deeds of others to the station. This would ensure that the effort is community driven, not based on what the station tells a community its civic needs should be. It would also apply to families; extra credits would be earned if parents and their children learn skills that are valuable to their community. A regular, on-air celebration of the accomplishments of Civic Certification would not only advance the message that this region cherishes community service, but also that the station is an advocate for such activity.

Idea 38

Organization: Community Recreation Center
Subject Area: Community – Recreation
Keyword Search: recreation, community recreation center, joggers, exercise, fitness

---

Strategy

Grow and support an increased quality of life. In addition, the center would work to "win back" or gain users from other facilities, attract users from out of the district, and adopt a more aggressive sales approach for services and products.

Underlying Value

The recreation center can use marketing strategies to carry the message to the public that it is a stalwart in the community, contributing substantially to the origin of the community's spirit of healthy living.

Components

The center could develop programs around three forms of incentives to save and make money, to meet social needs and to provide rewards.

Execution

Jogger's Map. The center could produce a map in partnership with a local hotel and distribute it to guests. This "Official Jogger's Map" of the area can include places of interest that the jogger will encounter along the way. The map will also generate money and public relations.

Exercise Calendar. The center could provide a seasonal calendar that program registrants can use for marking personal dates and health- or recreation-related events and goals. It would include class registration dates, activity tear-out pages and send-ins as well as customized content for corporate use if the order is large enough. The calendar can be pre-sold to area merchants and to social and civic groups that would use it to raise money for their organizations.

Executive Travel Health Fitness Kit. This collection of lightweight, flexible and portable items is designed for the executive traveler who does not enjoy running or does not take advantage of a hotel's facilities (if there are any). The kit would include items like a jump rope, an isometric device, water-filled weights, a massager, a tip sheet with exercises, and health information on the benefits of keeping in shape.

Birthday Promotion. This promotion rewards members on their birthday with a free day at the facility and/or discounts at the center's pro shop. It encourages continued exercise with age.

Crafts Fair. This annual event would feature the "best of" items produced at the center's craft classes. The items would be displayed and sold at a shopping mall, at the recreation center or during a larger community event (an outdoor festival, for example).

Annual Spring Sports Exchange. The exchange provides members with the opportunity to "swap" their old sporting goods for new ones. At the end of the event, the remaining used sports equipment would be sold at a profit, and a percentage of that profit would be donated to a designated community charity. An exchange entrance fee could provide an additional source of revenue.

Idea 39

Organization: Public Recreational Swimming Association
Subject Area: Community – Recreation
Keyword Search: aquatic centers, swim meets, competitions, sales kiosks

Strategy

Develop an organizational vision that transcends separate groups within the association, such as clubs, summer versus winter swimmers, competitive versus developmental swimmers, and water polo versus scuba diving.

Underlying Value

The association can better serve its members by developing a network of cooperating aquatic and recreation centers that participate in income-generating activities.

Components

Aquatics Sales Kiosks. This kiosk features hard goods that serve improved performance, fashion consciousness and other consumer interests of people engaged in aquatics. Merchandise would include privately labeled "Swim Association" clothing, towels, soaps, shampoos, foods and other useful items. Kiosks would be set up during events or competitions and during regular hours on peak attendance days at the cooperating swim and recreational centers.

The association could make the kiosk available to centers across the country that would provide their own staffing. Swim and recreation center managers would benefit by earning a profit for their organization and spending time with people and activities that are familiar and enjoyable. Some of the larger centers already sell items, but they are not visible or market oriented. Their customers would benefit by gaining greater access to useful products.

Execution

The association could act as a broker or organizer of a network. It would provide members with valuable access to corporate advertisers while returning a percentage of profits to the cooperating centers. As the umbrella organization for a "league" of cooperating aquatic and recreation centers, the association could also leverage its access to health enthusiasts. Corporations and other businesses would pay to gain access to the people who frequent aquatic and recreation centers.

Because this idea relies on the participation of center managers, the association must create an incentive plan to keep them motivated. Managers cannot be expected to sell actual products, so the rewards would be based on their passive participation at the minimum. For instance, a manager who wants minimal involvement would simply receive an annual fee for allowing the kiosk to remain in his center. Another manager may want to become more involved and therefore choose to receive income and free, high quality products for her users.

Idea 40

Organization: Public Swimming Association
Subject Area: Community – Recreation
Keyword Search: club swimming, competitive swimming, competitive diving, camp, water sports, surfing, scuba diving

Strategy

Create products and services for two distinct types of swimming participants–competitive and developmental–plus organized aquatic sports teams like water polo.

Underlying Value

The swimming association can become recognized as the umbrella organization for swim training, education and events by creating an aquatics university. This concept provides more to consumers than the typical courses and programs offered by most recreation centers.

Components

The aquatics university would create its own course of study, achievement levels and progression tracks. It could establish an annual camp-like experience at a highly respected swimming facility, offer advanced degrees to coaches in high tech training, or set new standards for coaching, diving, swimming, water polo, wind surfing, kayaking and administrative programs. The curriculum could include seminars on the latest swim research, demonstrations on techniques and new technology for coaches. Certificates of attendance and continuing education credits would be issued to the students.

Execution
The association can recruit its network of qualified coaches and staff to serve as faculty. These individuals may have experience ranging from an amateur swimming background to a youth counselor or administrator to a coach. Each staff member should have respectable credentials since his or her involvement lends credibility to the university and prestige to the image of the association.

Idea 41

Organization: Telecommunications Provider
Subject Area: Community – Human Relations
Keyword Search: tolerance, ethnic tolerance, healthy communication, telecommunications, phone

Strategy
Become known as the country's authority on and advocate for identifying and preventing social dysfunction that leads to inadequate communication and poor communication.

Underlying Value
If we want a more civil society, we must promote ethnic tolerance. As the country's premier telecommunications provider, this company is in a position to facilitate nationwide programs and activities that enable people to:
- Celebrate their uniqueness
- Interact with their neighbors
- Share their experiences
- Find common ground to improve relationships
- Promote tolerance and understanding.

Through this initiative, the company can move the needle closer to the reality of tolerance and understanding for citizens of every stripe.

Components

The Diverse Works Summit. This two-day summit could become a signature event for the company to use for launching its initiatives programs. It would unite the country's premier political, business and social leaders along with other citizen leaders in a call to action. The Diverse Works Summit, designed to increase understanding among diverse citizens, would build upon steps already being taken by the corporate partners and communities across the country.

The summit will consist of one thousand citizens formed into community teams with representatives from the private, public and not-for-profit sectors at both national and local levels. Participants would be invited to the capital to launch a strategy for citizen service and community leadership that can "turn the tide" on the social challenges facing so many communities today.

Organizations and institutions that are invited to the summit would be asked to make a tangible commitment to new activities that create the conditions necessary for increased tolerance and understanding. These could include:

- Education to promote awareness, appreciation and understanding of diversity among citizens
- Support for cultural celebrations and ethnic pride that leads to a reduction in crime and a rise in self-esteem among minority populations
- Supportive programs that offer realistic, practical solutions to real-life problems faced by working families, ethnic minorities, small businesses and retired citizens
- Inspiration and opportunities for individuals of every race and creed, young and old, to give back to others through community service.

Execution

Product Reward Pricing. This well-known method of selling more products or services features special pricing when people purchase more than one item. The company would reward new and existing customers who add products and services to their existing phone service (bundling the services together for a lower rate). The more products a customer subscribes to, or the more expensive the products, the more reduction or "reward" the company could offer. This pricing would generate goodwill through donations of a percentage of sales to the summit effort. It could be used as either a special promotion or an ongoing offer.

Gifts of Gab. People love to receive gifts, and they like to talk on the phone. Gifts of Gab would provide an intriguing way for the company to market products and services to current customers and to win new ones. Customers could purchase gift certificates for the company's hardware (telephones, cell phones or additional phone lines); services (conference calling, call waiting); or products (calling cards, cell phone accessories) for other customers. The gift items could increase the appeal of the company's products and services to existing customers and tempt others to become customers. The company could launch several targeted advertising campaigns during the year. In the spring, for example, it could coincide with the bridal and graduation season. Charitable gifts from a percentage of all sales add another great element to the Gifts of Gab. These funds would help pay for the summit.

Idea 42

Organization: Private Company
Subject Area: Community – Volunteerism
Keyword Search: volunteer, employee volunteerism, special event, community

Strategy

Create the tools to establish a "caring edge" instead of a "cutting edge" volunteerism program. With this idea, the company can use a highly visible set of initiatives to foster gains in market share, customer and employee loyalty, and to add value to company products. It can also build appreciation for the company's support of community service.

Underlying Value

Research by organizations such as Cone Communications and Hill and Knowlton proves that a consumer is more inclined to make purchases from a company that is associated with concerns he or she cares about. In other words, brand identification alone is declining in its importance to consumers. In addition to customer loyalty benefits, employees and vendors will appreciate the company's initiative in developing and maintaining this marketing edge.

Components

The World Record for Volunteering. This mediagenic event would position the company as an active leader in the promotion of volunteerism. Employees and other company representatives would work with the partnering nonprofit organization to achieve a *Guinness Book of World Records* listing for the greatest number of volunteer sign-ups in a twenty-four-hour period. Not only would communities benefit from higher numbers of available volunteers, but the event would be perceived as fun.

Execution

The World Record for Volunteering. The company could initiate a nationwide competition through public relations, marketing and advertising. This friendly competition between regions or cities would motivate volunteer sign-ups to put their own community in the lead. The company could track this level of interest and use each of the media to communicate the results. Media promotion of how the event translates to community contributions would be powerful. For example, a modest goal of one hundred thousand sign-ups could represent an equivalent contribution–motivated by the company's leadership–of more than three million dollars. Customers will likely respond to this news with intensified attraction to company products and services, as well as increased loyalty.

Idea 43

Organization: Private Company
Subject Area: Community – Volunteerism
Keyword Search: community service, volunteering, coffee table book

---

Strategy

Create the tools to establish a "caring edge" instead of a "cutting edge" volunteerism program. With this idea, the company can use a highly visible set of initiatives to foster gains in market share, customer and employee loyalty, and add value to company products with a nationally acknowledged appreciation for company support of the community service message. It could also create a gold standard of community service that is associated with this corporate brand.

Underlying Value

Research by organizations such as Cone Communications and Hill and Knowlton proves that a consumer is more inclined to make purchases from a company that is associated with concerns he or she cares about. In other words, brand identification alone is declining in its importance to consumers. In addition to customer loyalty benefits, employees and vendors will appreciate the company's initiative in developing and maintaining this marketing edge.

Components
In Honor of Community Service. This effective marketing idea puts the corporate name and brand before consumers in their own homes by publishing a coffee table book highlighting volunteerism. The attractive photographs in this book would feature people in service to their communities. It would highlight the partnering nonprofit organization as well as prominently feature the company as the corporate champion of service and community revitalization.

Execution
In Honor of Community Service. This coffee table publication presents several sales opportunities. It will be a natural point of purchase item for other events the company hosts or joins that are relevant to community service. It could also be used as a public television-related product, promoting a public television series on volunteering. Or, it could serve as a mail-in purchase opportunity for users of the call-to-action tools. The company could also benefit from retail sales of the book. A message printed on the cover or copyright page would alert readers that a portion of the proceeds from sales of the book will go to the participating nonprofit organization.

Idea 44
Organization: Nonprofit Disaster Relief Organization
Subject Area: Community – Volunteerism
Keyword Search: hometown, caring caravan, community, disaster relief, elderly

Strategy
Partner with a corporate sponsor to provide measurable benefits including the following:
- A number of useful and appealing products associated with the organization
- A stronger, more loyal relationship between the organization and its cor-

porate partners, their customers, employees and the public
- An enhanced reputation for the organization and its marketing partners
- A diversified income-generation program.

Underlying Value

The "Bringing Help, Bringing Hope to Your Hometown" initiative capitalizes on the nonprofit's reputation for brass tacks readiness in times of emergency. Products and services under this initiative provide means of community mobilization, family preparedness, and tools for helping others in one's own neighborhood. At its most basic form, caring starts in the home, and this community-building initiative provides resources to people so they can effectively care for one another.

Components

Community Mobilization. The organization could create a "Caring Caravan," an entourage of vans, emergency vehicles, eighteen-wheeler trucks, and other vehicles powered by volunteers and employees, all bearing the logos of the organization and its corporate partner. The caravan would bring medical treatment to the needy. It would also stand ready to present dramatizations of disaster relief and train anyone who is willing to volunteer the skills needed to help the community in an emergency.

Execution

Community mobilization can have multiple "arms and legs" including the following.

MASH Units. Over the past couple of years in several communities across America, the National Guard was mobilized to provide medical services to the homeless. Their tented clinics were a huge success, bringing much-needed immunizations, evaluations and emergency treatment to thousands of adults and children. But budget cuts closed these units. This has created a great opportunity for an organization and its corporate partners to step in. Not only could valuable services be provided, but community volunteers could be trained to be ready for emergencies in their own neighborhoods. These events would be so well received that positive publicity would also be an important outcome. In fact, if the units are packaged with a celebrity spokesperson and coordinated events at local schools and hospitals, they would become a full-scale media event.

Emergency Home Repair Corps. Trained by the organization's professional emergency response teams, these local citizens would be on call for small-scale emergencies in their hometowns. The corporation could provide help in the home when an elderly or disadvantaged person's fuse blows, water pipe breaks, or furnace needs cleaning for safety reasons. This team would be "at the ready," just like all of the organization's workers, but would have no inclination to take their show out of town.

Docu-Dramas. These videos or live events produced by the organization would offer training and insight into community-wide emergency preparedness needs. Training footage can be interspersed with video from the organization's efforts around the world. The footage should feature effective relief work and community mobilization enhanced by the organization's presence.

The videos could be purchased by cities for checkout from their public libraries. They could also be purchased in bulk by video retailers for modest rental fees or provided free as a community service. Dramas presented by professional actors in city plazas would intensify the value of a MASH unit visit and would build sales of the videos.

Idea 45

Organization: Private Company in the Home Repair Industry
Subject Area: Community – Volunteerism
Keyword Search: safe communities, youth, elder, employment, housing, resource center

Strategy

Establish the Old Pros, a corps of service clerks offering personalized services to customers. Also, staff a traveling educational program for seniors about home maintenance and repair.

Underlying Value

The company recognizes a commitment to building safer communities where both the youth and the elderly can gain independence, employment opportunities and adequate housing. These initiatives further that commitment in a way that is very visible to the general public.

Components

Old Pro Resource Center. Staffed by volunteers who are retired plumbers, electricians, craftsmen and contractors, this service center would be located in the company's home repair store. Old Pros would not only be available for advice; they would also act as personal shoppers who guide customers from question to register.

Execution

Old Pro Handyman Services. These volunteers would serve the community and act as company ambassadors of goodwill and good deeds. The company can accomplish this with a number of initiatives. In highly visible, specially marked vans, Old Pros could go to homes of seniors and low-income residents to do repairs. Pros could also teach self-help home repair to youth, seniors and other low-income housing tenants as part of a traveling home maintenance and repair educational program.

In addition, representatives could attend community events such as block parties, 4-H craft fairs, neighborhood festivities and energy fairs. Furthermore, in partnership with a local nonprofit, the Old Pros could donate their time and service to a home building project, or complete maintenance on a building, school, museum or other facility.

Idea 46
Organization: Private Company
Subject Area: Community – Volunteerism
Keyword Search: caring, community service, 900 number

Strategy

Create the tools to establish a "caring edge" (not "cutting edge") volunteerism program through a private company interested in community service. With this idea, the company can employ a highly visible set of initiatives to foster gains in market share as well as customer and employee loyalty, and add value to the company's products with a nationally acknowledged appreciation for company support of the community service message.

Underlying Value

Research by organizations such as Cone Communications and Hill and Knowlton proves that a consumer is more inclined to make purchases from a company that is associated with concerns he or she cares about. In other words, brand identification alone is declining in its importance to consumers. In addition to customer loyalty benefits, employees and vendors will appreciate the company's initiative in developing and maintaining this marketing edge.

Components

The Community Service 900 Number. Many Americans complain that one of the main reasons they do not contribute their time and talents to their communities is that it is so difficult to find an organization or project that matches their schedules. Each component of this strategy would introduce citizens to this service, branded with the company name, which offers specific, individualized information on organizations in a specific area that need volunteers.

Execution

The Community Service 900 Number. This could be structured as a profit-generating mechanism by making the service a 900 number. Under this scenario, the company would publicize that a portion of the proceeds from use of the Community Service 900 number will be donated to the organization. A 900 number targets the number one sales strategy of modern time: Americans will pay for convenience, and they are much more likely to pay for a service if an organization in which they believe will benefit from their purchase.

Education

Idea 47

Organization: International School
Subject Area: Education – Cultural Awarenesss
Keyword Search: education, international, peace, diversity, transition, youth, family

Strategy

Become an international standard setter in education. Develop and market products, services, promotions and programs that uphold this new standard and serve the needs of the corporate partner(s).

Underlying Value

This initiative can only be successful with a commitment from a corporate partner. The school should approach a partner that has an affinity for global issues that involve peace and diversity. It should also try to choose an international company that seems ripe for these or similar business propositions.

Components

As an international school, two themes arise to support the strategy. These include:
- Peace – With a history of involvement in international peace issues, the school is positioned to embrace this as a major theme. Moreover, the school has a keen interest in and resources available for promoting peace for children in a family context.
- Diversity – This includes cultural and geographic diversity as well as the study of geography. The school is a natural extension of the study of the global environment.

Execution

Peace Dolls. Nobel Prize winners in doll form are dolls with a purpose. Each comes with a book, describing what the winner did to earn the award. A variation might be kids under eighteen who have done something extraordinary in this area.

Peace Fantasy Camps. Participants could pay to attend a summer camp with retired and active diplomats. They would learn how to mediate disputes in their families, their work, or their child's local sports association. Sessions could be run by diplomats, current United Nations personnel and families of the diplomatic personnel.

The Peace Prize. This prestigious award could honor children who respect peace and have demonstrated it in their lives. This would include a strict selection process and extensive media coverage.

International Costumes. The goal would be to resemble a person from another country and educate others about the culture of a child from another country. The costumes could come complete with jewelry and books or audio recordings that contain stories and lessons about the culture. The costume could be sold through major retailers or international children's agencies.

International Etiquette. These books, posters, compact discs or tapes would tell people the appropriate etiquette in various countries. Topics could include when to use napkins, what to eat, how to eat certain foods, or what to do when you meet an older person, a younger person, an authority figure or one of your peers. The school could develop separate versions for adults and for kids, with a common focus on families.

International Teleconference on Youth Choices. This could be a conference through a satellite hookup between a central location and down-linked sights around the world. The international school would host the teleconference to the best and brightest young minds worldwide for a fee. Discussion topics could range from world peace to fashion, education and environmental issues.

A Children's World Fair. This regular event would celebrate international young people, their potential, accomplishments and ability to share in developing human potential. Geared toward children under the age of eighteen, this fair would include foods, crafts, games and friend-making. Exhibitors at the fair could include anyone with an international position, such as language schools, ethnic restaurants, multi-national corporations and airlines. The school could create booths representing individual countries, so children interested in visiting a certain country could go to the booth to meet someone who is from that country or is representing it. The school could also host an international film festival that shows some of the best films about children around the world.

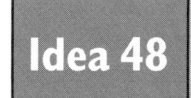

Idea 48

Organization: Private School
Subject Area: Education – Cultural Awareness
Keyword Search: international, student exchange programs, cultural exchange

---

Strategy
Position a private academic academy as an upbeat, proactive, national pacesetter in education. Advance international and inter-cultural understanding and cooperation.

Underlying Value
Since it is a private school, the academy has the ability to "think outside the box," an essential component to reaching across cultures and international boundaries. Their nationally prominent Centers for International Understanding would teach both children and adults global awareness and a respect for diverse cultures.

Components
Center for International Understanding. The center would develop services and

events that highlight the connections among all nationalities. Other schools, companies and nonprofit organizations could emulate these interactive, practical experiences or adopt them for a fee once the academy has licensed them.

Execution
Student or Class Exchange. The academy could initiate an exchange program with schools in another part of the city, the country or the world in which individual students can exchange locations for a limited period of time. If the exchange takes place locally, whole classes can exchange places.

Parent or Family Exchange. The academy could initiate a program in which parents or whole families can exchange locations with parents or families in another country.

Teacher Exchange. The school could initiate a program in which one or more academy teachers trade places with a teacher in a foreign school every year.

International Institute. Another blockbuster exchange could be between children or grandchildren of world leaders. The children would be invited to a one-week symposium to discuss major world issues. It would be underwritten by corporate sponsors and registration fees. The academy would receive national, and possibly international, recognition for initiating a program of this kind.

Idea 49

Organization: Institute for Citizenship, Democracy and Leadership for Young Adults
Subject Area: Education – Citizenship
Keyword Search: leadership, youth, tolerance, courage, democracy, kiosks, citizenship

---

Strategy
Become the premier training and education authority on citizenship and leadership among young adults, and provide vision and hope for a better future.

Underlying Value
The company who brings knowledge, understanding and a vision for the future to young adults builds a bridge to its own future. This alliance with the institute

will show the company's customers that they care about high quality leadership, dedication to tolerance, and living by courage and conviction.

Components
This idea positions the organization as a tremendous resource for information in the advancement of democracy and justice via cutting edge delivery systems. This will also serve consumers with practical information.

Execution
Street Law Kiosks. This initiative captures people while they wait–at the airport, bus stop or mall, for example. The computerized kiosk would provide information about conflict resolution, human rights and the advancement of democracy, based on years of research and development achieved by the organization. The corporate partner would gain a captive audience, plus an opportunity to promote its products on each printout.

Idea 50

Organization: Private School
Subject Area: Education – Creativity
Keyword Search: private educational academy, education, children's book, competitions, creativity, imagination

---

Strategy
Position a private academic academy as an upbeat, proactive, national pacesetter in education.

Underlying Value
Creating a nationally prominent center for creativity and imagination will promote the original thinking that leads to practical inventions. This initiative translates fresh ideas into products and raises awareness of the school's unique offerings.

Components
Center for Creativity and Imagination. The academy can become the "Home

of Original Thinking," starting with two competitions.

Inventions Competition – This city-wide contest challenges people in several categories to invent a device that serves a purpose, such as:
- A device that saves money
- A device that saves energy
- An educational toy
- A new computer game.

The competition should be underwritten by a corporation and extend the academy's "Challenge to Excellence" to the rest of the community.

Children's Book Competition – This local competition invites children between the ages of six and eighteen to write, design and produce a children's book. For fairness, the entries should be divided by age group: six to eight, nine to eleven, twelve to fifteen and sixteen to eighteen. Winning entries could go on display at a local bookstore, which might also serve as an event sponsor.

Execution

Because of the aggressive nature of the proposed programs, the school should use two approaches to funding–a traditional development method and a less conventional earned income or programmatic method. The approach should capitalize on parent gifts as well as alumni gifts. The school would appoint or hire a director of enterprise or director of business development who would report directly to the head supervisor. In concert with the faculty and administration, he or she would shepherd and monitor all aspects of the academy's development.

Idea 51

Organization: Private School
Subject Area: Education – Family Involvement
Keyword Search: private school education, parenting skills, resource center, preschoolers

Strategy

Position the private academy as an upbeat, proactive pacesetter in education by creating a nationally prominent Center for Confident Parenting.

Underlying Value

The school is uniquely qualified to create the parenting center because of its educational history, environment and resources. The center would make many philosophical statements about learning and education primarily through its existence and ultimately through its programs. One such statement is that parents are frontline educators. The atmosphere in the center would convey the conviction that parents, teachers and students are partners in the learning process.

Components

Parenting Center. This center would be a multifaceted effort that integrates many of the highest priority program components. It would give the academy a chance to reach those families who cannot come to it due to distance, physical limitations or other problems. In both on-campus programs and satellite center programs, courses on all aspects of education and parenting would be offered to the general public.

Programs would take place at various times of the day, with a heavy emphasis on evening and weekend programs. Course content could focus on issues not being addressed elsewhere, especially social issues that affect the family. Some subjects might include:

- Constructive television watching
- Violence in the world
- Sex and drugs
- Divorce
- The successful family
- Homework and study habits
- Preparing for tests
- Using the computer
- Navigating the Internet (what sites to visit and which to avoid)
- Helping your child achieve
- Choosing college
- Death in the family and terminal illness
- Single parent families
- Working parents
- Handling handicaps
- Saying no to potentially dangerous situations

- Choosing a day care center
- Choosing a summer camp.

Course sessions could be videotaped with broadcast rights sold to cable television. Course content could also be published in a book.

In time, satellite centers might be created off campus in the evenings and on weekends. The center could be set up in rented space at other schools, churches or meeting places that are convenient for the target audiences. Satellite centers are not recommended in the first three years except on a very limited trial basis so that center's existence is not compromised while it gets its program working well.

Execution

Family Computer Mini-Institute. The institute might serve many functions. It can test new software for use in schools and teach practical, hands-on courses in computer skills, such as how to use a home computer. The institute can also serve as a live testing ground for Internet sites geared to children and families who want to get usability feedback. Internet companies can pay a fee to have families "surf" their sites and complete this evaluation form.

Tips from "Your Academy." The academy's teachers are already developing innovative, proven curriculum materials for use in their own classrooms. Creating and packaging the curriculum as kits for use by parents or public school teachers would be a great way to generate funds for the school. Kits could include not only lessons teaching essential concepts in math, science and composition, but also units covering specific eras in social studies, literature, or art. Academy-designed sets of at-home activity cards could enhance the kits. They could be advertised in the local school magazine, or sold through local stores and the Parenting Center. The sale price would reflect a profit to the businesses and to the academy, which could be shared with the teachers who supplied ideas for the cards.

Moms and Tots. There is a tremendous need for educating the mothers of preschool aged children. This very large audience is looking for educational activities to complete with their children during the days. The academy can meet this need by offering educational, daytime workshops for moms and tots.

Idea 52

Organization: Private School
Subject Area: Education – Young Entrepreneurs
Keyword Search: international, student exchange programs, cultural exchange

Strategy

Position a private children's academy as an upbeat, proactive, national pacesetter in education by creating opportunities for children to learn business skills and become entrepreneurs.

Underlying Value

Preparing children for adulthood should include teaching them skills for their chosen occupation. Entrepreneurial skills benefit the students who will lead the businesses and other organizations of the future. The academy values these skills and considers itself a leader in shaping tomorrow's leaders.

Components

Center for Youth Enterprise. Underwritten by a corporation, this curriculum would focus on teaching entrepreneurial, real world skills to children. All instruction would include a focus on developing one's creativity. The children would learn skills such as calculated risk taking, problem solving, and trust of their intuition. The center would create a number of recommendations and time them for maximum impact.

Execution

A Yellow Pages for Kids. This project allows children to learn concepts such as research, packaging, pricing, sales strategy, pre-selling and distribution. It would create a vested interest among students if a "profit sharing plan" were established during the planning stages. These would not be childish publications; they would be polished, professional and appealing to adults.

"The Academy" Student Employment Service. Junior high and high school students are frequently looking for jobs. This student-run employment agency would meet that need. At the same time, it would give these agency "employees" valuable business experience.

Great American Lemonade Stand. (See Idea 11) This business idea, though tried and true, is new to some children. The project would include an emphasis on advancing the child's business skills.

Scholar in Residence. Each year, the academy would bring in a well-known writer, playwright, artist, philosopher, economist or other leader to hold classes and workshops on a regular basis with students, faculty and parents. Evening sessions could be open to the general public for an admission fee. If underwritten by a corporation, this could be the "X" Corporation Scholar in Residence Program. The public relations and income potential are high.

Environment

Idea 53

Organization: Horse (Breeders, Owners and Enthusiasts) Association
Subject Area: Environment – Animals
Keyword Search: horse, police, character, breed, service, animal, pet

Strategy
Increase awareness among the general public of the multiple values surrounding a certain horse breed. Through a sustainable, mutually beneficial partnership with a corporation, further the organization's goal of meeting members' horse ownership needs.

Underlying Value
This association is based on the ideals of quality, character, discipline and compassion. As a member society, it has worked for generations to promote a specific

breed of horse because of its remarkable equine characteristics. The breed is an intelligent animal with tremendous strength, combined with a gentle spirit and a consistently affectionate personality.

Components

The association will develop initiatives that educate children and adults in a fun and practical way. These initiatives will increase awareness of the organization and further promote the value of horse ownership.

Execution

Breeding Good Character. The qualities of this breed are a refreshing metaphor for what matters to many people today. Regardless of their experience with horses, these individuals know that quality moral character is something that is built over time–often over many generations. The Breeding Good Character initiative could provide the corporate partner with an excellent opportunity to reach attractive market segments with the message that this company cares about strengthening the moral integrity of the next generation of our nation's leaders. Students would learn about the qualities of loyalty, flexibility, patience and leadership that this horse breed exhibits. They would also realize that they can develop these characteristics as well.

Quality Character Cards. Police departments in many cities give kids trading cards with their officers' pictures and information to build positive identification with law enforcement. Similarly, the association could help produce cards with pictures of this specific breed of park police horses. These cards would feature a photo and interesting facts about this particular animal. It would engage kids with the message: "This animal has qualities we all need to build a better future. Remember the horse when you think about the kind of person you want to be."

Park Police Partners. This program would bring the Breeding Good Character theme into schools. The association would coordinate visits by mounted police officers, most of whom ride this breed with great pride. These officers would describe how the horses provide them with the characteristics they need most in an animal partner: loyalty, intelligence, strength and other qualities that translate well to humans. This helps teachers, parents and children recognize these horses as the gentle giants they see serving the community.

Idea 54

Organization: Horse (Breeders, Owners and Enthusiasts) Association
Subject Area: Environment – Animals
Keyword Search: horses, pet ownership, responsible, animal care, pet relationship, compost

Strategy
Increase awareness among the general public of the multiple values surrounding a certain horse breed. Through a sustainable, mutually beneficial partnership with a corporation, further the organization's goal of meeting members' horse ownership needs.

Underlying Value
This association is based on the ideals of quality, character, discipline and compassion. As a member society, it has worked for generations to promote a specific breed of horse because of its remarkable equine characteristics. The breed is an intelligent animal with tremendous strength, combined with a gentle spirit and a consistently affectionate personality.

Components
Responsible Pet Ownership Program. This association represents owners who are dedicated to their horses. But, it can also serve as an excellent resource for promoting disciplined and loving ownership of all types of pets. This program could allow the association to educate and inform its own members, while continuing to offer products and services to best care for a horse. It could also speak to owners of other equine breeds as well as owners of the average dog, cat or rabbit. This would allow a corporate partner to help set the national standard and serve as a valuable resource in promoting the value and responsibility of pet ownership.

Execution
Get a Good Start with Your Pet. The message of this initiative is that the association and its corporate partner are prepared to set a national standard for pet ownership. When someone adopts a pet from a shelter, pet store or other place, they would receive "goodies" from various manufacturers and service providers. The package would not be branded, nor would it be coordinated

to provide information on what it means to be a good pet owner. The main focus would be helping the owner to get the most out of the relationship with the pet. The kit would provide coupons on food and other items, toys, and general tips about animals.

Good Start Affinity Programs. This program is modeled on a successful promotion for new babies and new parents. The association and its partner would gather names of new pet owners from shelters, pet stores and breeders. After these new "parents" receive the "Get a Good Start with Your Pet Kit," they would receive a new toy and information packet each month following the adoption. Unless the pet owners return the merchandise or call to cancel, they will be billed every month for each new shipment. To motivate pet owners to continue with the program, every package retained and every billing paid would trigger donations to high quality animal protection programs.

Animal Care Curriculum. Many educators know that children who own pets and learn to take good care of them are often more skilled at taking care of other life responsibilities. For this reason, many elementary school teachers keep a classroom gerbil or snake so students can practice serving the needs of a relatively helpless animal.

The association could prepare a curriculum that covers animal care issues. It would help teachers present lessons on discipline, nutrition, understanding the natural needs of an animal, and concern for the animal kingdom, including our responsibility to protect all creatures. In book, compact disc or video form, this curriculum would present an excellent joint venture opportunity for a feed manufacturer or national veterinary association.

Classy Compost. Just as it sounds, this product would be sold as "Classy Compost" to benefit wildlife programs. The manure-based compost could be sold to promote horse-related charitable activities. The association and its corporate partner would market Classy Compost through nurseries and garden centers. Consumers that use this product would be triggering donations to programs such as wild horse rescue, handicapped riding or the Park Police Partners program (see Idea 52).

Service with Your Pet Program. This concept links the themes of responsible pet ownership and breeding good character. The catalog developed for the program would describe opportunities for the owners of all kinds of animals to volunteer in a setting where pets are valued. Settings could include nursing homes, homeless shelters, psychiatric hospitals, day care centers, elder care centers, juvenile detention facilities and hospices. It could be offered to consumers free with a donation to the association. The association would be seen as the facilitator of yet another rewarding dimension of pet ownership, as well as a caring organization in the community.

> **Idea 55**
> **Organization:** Horse (Breeders, Owners and Enthusiasts) Association
> **Subject Area:** Environment – Animals
> **Keyword Search:** bloodline, heritage, historic trails, horses

Strategy
Increase awareness among the general public of the multiple values surrounding a certain horse breed. Through a sustainable, mutually beneficial partnership with a corporation, further the organization's goal of meeting members' horse ownership needs.

Underlying Value
This association is based on the ideals of quality, character, discipline and compassion. As a member society, it has worked for generations to promote a specific breed of horse because of its remarkable equine characteristics. The breed is an intelligent animal with tremendous strength, combined with a gentle spirit and a consistently affectionate personality.

Components
Preserving the Best of our Past. This project offers the corporation an opportunity to position itself as an advocate for preservation of national treasures, including animal life. The organization works to preserve a breed because it has great beauty and a rich heritage from which a lot can be learned. With this breed of horses comes the strength of the best bloodlines.

Execution
Preservation Products. The association could directly sell a line of products that help preserve things that matter to Americans. Or, it could work with

manufacturers to sell items such as saddle soaps that protect cherished leather goods.

Another product could be a series of scrapbooks and photo albums designed to preserve personal memorabilia in much the same way that horse owners save ribbons, records and genealogical histories of their horses. The association would target those consumers who perceive their possessions as things that matter and who work to keep them in excellent condition. These preservation efforts would also serve the consumer's desire to preserve things that matter to an entire community or nation.

Historic Trails Project. Many of the trails that people know as walking or biking paths were originally highways for horses. This project could be created in partnership with a "rails to trails" organization (which works to transform old railroad beds into paved foot and bike paths) or a company interested in innovative outdoor projects. The association would preserve its own set of trails that were once the means of transportation for horses and their owners with funding support from its corporate partners.

Association members could get involved through trail construction or donations, and gain the added benefit of building a community identity for horse owners. Each of these preserved trails would feature signs and plaques that detail how the trail was originally used. Signs would also describe the interesting citizens and horses that traversed it through the years.

Idea 56

Organization: International Agriculture Research Organization
Subject Area: Environment – Biodiversity
Keyword Search: environment, ecosystems, agriculture, hunger, patents, poverty, biodiversity

Strategy

Raise the profile of the organization, increase awareness of its social-economic-environmental mission among the broadest range of constituents, and provide it with a sustainable stream of income. Most importantly, create a program that enables the average citizen to become a hero for individuals who are living in poverty.

Underlying Value

This concept recognizes and responds to the alarming fact that the rich have become richer as the poor have become more desperate. This gap creates an additional problem; affluent groups of people have a voracious appetite for goods that are produced at the expense of ecosystems in the developing world. The purchasing behaviors of consumers, whether they realize it or not, contribute to world hunger. Consumers would prefer to know that their choice to a buy particular product is helping to alleviate poverty and protect the earth–not the opposite. "Growing Wealthy" provides the corporate partner with an ideal opportunity to promote its investment in developing countries as well as its investment in one of the most viable agricultural and economic opportunities for impoverished nations.

Components

Patents for the Poor. Today, when a transnational corporation files for protection of a patent, it retains proprietary ownership of the critical information that leads to the sale of a product. International patent law currently allows that corporation to benefit from its research investment for seven years. After that, the information is considered public domain; anyone can then sell products that were made using that information. The Growing Wealthy initiative would partner the corporations with patent-worthy information and the international bodies that offer patent protection. Together, they would direct a percentage of the profits generated by the patent to the organization's programs in countries where the proprietary information originated.

A variety of agriculture patents could be included, allowing significant funding to reach the organization's programs that alleviate hunger in developing nations.

Execution

In one example, a pharmaceutical company may use agricultural data produced by the organization's researchers to develop a drug for which it seeks patent protection. Patents for the Poor would enable the company to enjoy a longer period of patent protection once it agrees to share royalties from sales of that drug with the organization.

Idea 57

Organization: International Agriculture Research Organization
Subject Area: Environment – Biodiversity
Keyword Search: agriculture, crops, sustainable, earth, planting, seeds

Strategy

Raise the profile of the organization, increase awareness of its social-economic-environmental mission among the broadest range of constituents, and provide it with a sustainable stream of income. Most important, enable the average citizen to become a hero for individuals who are living in poverty.

Underlying Value

This organization is best suited to put a human face on the global problems of insufficient food sources and ecological degradation. Through this initiative, corporate partners could deliver a "down to earth" message that consumers can understand. With a common focus in view, they would be motivated to work with the company to make a real difference for hungry people across the developing world.

Despite technological advances that deliver information from around the world almost instantaneously, citizens of the world's wealthiest societies usually do not see a human face when asked to think of the developing world. This initiative would link the organization's agricultural development efforts with real people who do not have enough to eat and whose homelands are being destroyed by irresponsible environmental practices. The agricultural research organization would enable an average consumer to invest in agricultural programs in the third world. Their investment would aim to alleviate food shortages not just for a day, but for as long as it takes to assure that children never again suffer from hunger.

Components

Seeds of Promise. Each purchase of the corporation's products could generate a donation to the organization which would then provide food for the world's hungry people by planting sustainable and environmentally sound crops. In addition, consumers could purchase a hybrid seed and name it. The consumers' purchase would offer them the opportunity to help feed thousands of people in an impoverished community.

Execution
Seeds of Promise. Individuals who want to buy a gift for the "person who has everything" could buy a Seed of Promise to honor that person. The gift acknowledges the connection between two people and their shared commitment to sensible agricultural practices and the alleviation of poverty.

Grandparents could purchase Seeds of Promise for their grandchildren and later show them through reports from the organization how their seed was planted in a third world country, leading to sustainable crops and income generation for the people of that region. The program could be marketed on Web sites, in home improvement centers, in nurseries and in other businesses associated with horticulture or agriculture.

Idea 58
Organization: International Agriculture Research Organization
Subject Area: Environment – Biodiversity
Keyword Search: hunger, food, organic, environment, sustainable

Strategy
Raise the profile of the organization and increase awareness of its social-economic-environmental mission among the broadest range of constituents. Also, provide the organization with a sustainable stream of income. Most importantly, enable the average citizen to become a hero for individuals who are living in poverty.

Underlying Value
Brain Food. This initiative links intelligent thinking with positive, practical actions to alleviate hunger and protect the earth's resources. It also creates a connection between purchasing organic or "natural" products and making

a difference for the world's poorest populations. Products could include food, clothing, pharmaceuticals, furniture and manufactured goods. The vast majority of consumer products in this country can be linked to a plant or crop that grows in the third world. In addition to educating the consumer about products, this initiative could ignite a desire to know more about other parts of our planet.

Components

The Organization Private Label. With so many options on store shelves, how does a consumer know which one to choose? Most often, the label is a prime deciding factor. The private label underscores the idea that purchasing a product that supports the organization's programs is indeed a unique choice. Similar to the seals of approval used by other companies, the private label sends a message about a high standard of quality.

On one level, organization products would be designated "natural" or "organic." On a second level, the brand would represent products that give consumers extra purchasing power through the investment in organization programs. On a third level–because the label would include information on agricultural development in poor nations–the brand would represent a line of products that educates consumers about our planet and sustainability.

Execution

Gourmet Foods. These products would feature a "Top of the Crop" tag line that identifies them as quality items that are attractive to many food manufacturers, wholesalers and retailers. The organization would add a special endorsement of products made not only from sustainable crops, but also from the purest seed varieties.

Products for Children. This dimension of the private label initiative through the corporate partner could send this message: "Buy this product and your children will learn about innovative rice production in the Bouake Region of the Ivory Coast of Africa." The labels, shelf talkers and advertising would educate the children of affluent consumers that these products are made in specific countries, by people of specific nationalities or customs with agriculturally sound practices.

Idea 59

Organization: Public Garden
Subject Area: Environment – Biodiversity
Keyword Search: organically grown produce, backyard, seeds, plants, children, family

Strategy
Educate the public on the devastating effects that the loss of endangered plants will have on the ecosystem through a campaign called "The Panda in Your Back Yard."

Underlying Value
Unlike saving an endangered species in a faraway land, such as the panda bear in Asia, this strategy encourages actions individuals can take every day to improve the situation. The goal is not to make people feel guilty about events over which they have little control.

Components
This campaign offers consumers the ability to be proactive when they make purchases at the nursery, plant store or supermarket where they regularly shop. Through an educational outreach to children, the organization could urge parents to:
- Buy fruits and vegetables in season with the help of a chart that hangs on the refrigerator. This leads to a greater respect for nature's cycles and places less importance on species whose main characteristic is that they ship well.
- Choose little-known varieties of fruits and vegetables over better-known ones. This helps to increase the demand for varieties that might otherwise be in danger of dying out. Apples and squash are two examples of produce that come in many varieties.
- Select organically grown produce.
- Save heirloom seeds to grow in home gardens.
- Grow unusual varieties of plants, flowers, fruits and vegetables.

Execution
Products, Services and Memberships to Buy. Character items could include every-

116 / Cold Cash for Warm Hearts

thing from dolls to small plastic giveaway figures, T-shirts, mugs shaped like the characters or salad bowls with figures. Some examples are:
- Refrigerator chart with seasons for different fruits and vegetables
- Heirloom seed packets with gardening implements
- Pre-printed shopping list that features produce that is in season
- Cookbook featuring recipes that use lesser known varieties of fruits and vegetables
- Refrigerator magnets with environmentally sensitive messages as reminders
- Seeds and a character-decorated flower pot packaged together.

Membership in the "Rescuers League." By becoming members of this group, children ages six to twelve years old and their families would receive a number of premiums:
- Figure merchandise
- Seeds, tools and a pot in which to grow them
- A newsletter with recipes, puzzles and a shopping list for items that are in season or need to be planted that month
- A certificate and "Seed Rescue Badge" stating "I Rescued a Seed"
- A gardening apron
- A chart to map seeds from their early family history in other countries–a "family plant" similar to a family tree.

Idea 60

Organization: Nonprofit Conservation Organization
Subject Area: Environment – Biodiversity
Keyword Search: wildlife, tree swing, environment, earth, cooking classes

Strategy
Deliver conservation support to individuals and organizations around the world "on the ground" where it is most urgently needed.

Underlying Value
The success of communicating this organization's mission depends on link-

ing the past with the present and the future. The organization brings hope for effective preservation efforts to future generations in part by touching people emotionally and sensually through animal and plant stories, and visual presentations while stimulating their memories of firsthand contact. This initiative links the role of nature to us and our day-to-day lives. It also offers practical information to make life better for our children, our families, our homes and our gardens.

Components
The Organization X Tree Swing. This product would be sold in home centers, garden supply shops or casual furniture stores. Hanging tags could tell consumers that the swing is made from sustainable materials. It would also comment on memories of relaxing afternoons spent lounging in the shade, appreciating the protection and movement of a magnificent tree. The organization would emphasize that trees do indeed bring us pleasure and that our gift in return should be to preserve them for eternity.

Plush Toys. Many environmental organizations have successfully sold stuffed animal toys to generate revenue. The uniqueness of this idea is that the organization and its toy-manufacturing partner would feature "vulnerables," or animals in danger of extinction. This name recognizes a child's sense that he or she, too, is vulnerable to how adults treat our environment. The toy line could also feature animals that live in certain trees, providing the organization with an opportunity to educate consumers about plants that are vulnerable to extinction.

Tantalizing Scents. Marketed with beauty industry partners, these oils would come from plants that have been preserved at "peak fragrance." This product would definitely be linked to the current popularity of aromatherapy. Marketing strategies might include selling these as collector's items, offering consumers a chance to "keep" fragrances from endangered plants forever.

Cooking Classes. In kitchen stores or via video production, the organization would teach consumers to care about the earth through their cooking practices. The goal is to choose food products that are grown in the most sustainable manner possible.

Execution
This "Profiting from the Earth" set of financial mechanisms offers an ideal

opportunity for a corporate partner in banking or related industries.

Insurance. Customers could be offered the chance to check off an additional amount on their insurance policy renewal contracts, raising premium costs minimally and triggering donations to the organization.

Public Purpose Investment Bonds. Another proven mechanism, this idea could allow investors to participate in a vehicle with attractive financial returns while allocating fifty percent of the investment and its generated interest to the organization.

Charity Checks. A bank partner that prints personalized checks for its customers would offer them the chance to purchase this type, which includes a pre-printed check already inscribed with a donation to the organization. In this way, the bank offers a reminder to make a regular contribution to the organization's valuable programs. The charity check could be placed in one of every tenth, fiftieth or one hundredth check in a sequence, depending on the customer's preference.

Idea 61

Organization: Wine Manufacturer
Subject Area: Environment – Recycling
Keyword Search: wine, vineyards, conservation, planet, endangered wildlife, cork recycling

Strategy
Become known as the champion of living celebrations; of an appreciation for the natural world and the human family, and our nation's past, present and future. This company will be known for its dedication to encouraging those aspects of society that transform mere existence into an exuberant experience of life.

Underlying Value
With a reputation for producing fine wines, this company already has established itself as an advocate for environmental issues. This program focuses on the positive outcomes of caring for the earth and celebrating our future as inhabitants of this beautiful planet. It would build upon intangibles such as pride and respect, and encourage a sense of belonging.

Components

Adopt a Vineyard. This opportunity allows consumers to achieve two goals simultaneously. They can contribute to conservation efforts and find the perfect gift for the man or woman who has everything. In return they receive a deed that identifies the purchaser as the co-owner of a vineyard or orchard. In reading the fine print, the purchaser will discover that he or she is the owner of a square meter or even just a square centimeter.

However, the point is that, for a modest price, one can indeed claim to own a winery. Proceeds from the sale of these deeds will fund conservation efforts, like soil erosion and water pollution projects, that improve or preserve the natural resources needed for growing fruit. Anyone with a sincere interest in his or her investment will receive updates on the conservation efforts, plus discount coupons on future product purchases.

Execution

Packaging. Local residents are passionate about the diverse wildlife and ecosystems of the region where this vineyard is located. At the same time, many individuals seek practical ways to make a difference for the natural world, like purchasing products that directly support conservation. This vineyard could create a series of labels that feature treasured animal species or places of natural wonder for specially marketed wines. Purchase of these vintages would trigger a donation by the company to a fund for conservation efforts. Different family brands could "adopt" specific species or sites, perhaps based on ties to the local landscape.

The Company X Cork Recycling Program. Through displays in liquor stores, wine buyers would be encouraged to collect corks and then return them by mail to the company in pre-addressed envelopes available at the checkout counter. They could also be encouraged to deliver the corks directly to a vineyard. In return for recycling corks from any bottle of wine (not just their bottle), the consumer would receive a discount coupon on future purchases. Participants would also have the satisfaction of knowing that the recycled cork has been ground up into landscape material for nature trails at parks and beaches throughout the country.

The recycling program can be extended to impact sales of company brands in restaurants. A restaurant that collects corks would receive a discount on its next order. It could then pass that discount on to its wine-buying customers with a credit that states, "Thank you for participating in our partnership with Company X Wines to conserve our natural resources. Please redeem this coupon for ten percent off your next dinner with us."

Idea 62

Organization: Packaged Goods Manufacturer
Subject Area: Environment – Sustainability
Keyword Search: crop productivity, crops, food, earth, peanut butter, poverty

---

Strategy

The marketing strategy for this international company is based on effectively and consistently improving profitability by:
- Embracing the opportunities offered by global marketing
- Creating innovative strategies to capture a market share from competitors
- Increasing awareness of meaningful and culturally sensitive investments wherever the company has a presence.

Underlying Value

Particularly in complex economic situations, the company could benefit significantly from a "big idea." It would realize a marketing strategy that addresses globalization issues, competitor activities, and consumer and shareholder demand for significant investment in socially responsible activities. A big idea would offer an effective response to other risks to the company's reputation and strengthen its position as a family of brands worthy of the highest respect and loyalty.

Components

Down to Earth Initiative. This initiative tells consumers that they can make a "down to earth" difference among the world's less fortunate individuals by taking advantage of the company's investment in its public purpose marketing partner.

The initiative would illustrate how the partner's agricultural development efforts help real people build better lives in the developing world. For example, it would describe the process of reversing the destruction to homelands that are damaged by irresponsible environmental practices. When consumers purchase the company's products, they would discover that they are making a difference for children and families who deserve our active compassion.

This big idea could be supported through a partnership with a global nonprofit organization dedicated to increasing crop productivity, bringing about food security, reducing poverty and protecting the environment in the semi-arid, tropical regions of the world. The organization would send the message that it believes that its agricultural research should be judged not just on the quality of science but on how effectively the organization helps people escape from subsistence farming to achieve a better life. The partnership would position the company as the only marketer of the food product, while working to actively educate people about protecting the environment and reducing poverty around the world. A secondary benefit would be access to quality food products at reduced cost.

Execution

Where Does Peanut Butter Come From? The "Peanut Journey" would tell how peanuts start as seeds and end up in a jar on the shelf. This booklet would be offered free with the purchase of company products. It could serve as an end-cap theme and shelf talker in supermarkets and provide content for advertising the brand.

Parents are the primary targets of this mechanism. The company would offer to help children understand how and where peanuts are grown, and how this crop is essential to feeding children in poor communities around the world. Parents will appreciate how the company linked a product American kids love to a social message. Elements of this mechanism could be timed to coincide with peanut butter products or packaging innovations launched by competitors.

It could also be produced as an interactive story on the Internet. A similar product on the Web that explains the role of cotton has attracted thousands of children every week. Since the site is educational, teachers often use it as an interactive learning tool.

Peanut Butter Paint. This creative idea should appeal to every child's desire to play with his or her food. Six small, plastic containers of peanut butter–each a different color–could be packaged together. Every day as the child helps her mom or dad make lunch, she can choose a color for the peanut butter and jelly sandwich. Peanut Butter Paint could be packaged with stories of how these colors are represented in the developing world and what life is like for children in those places. Stories written and illustrated by professionals could also be included, educating American children while offering an entertaining twist to the mundane task of making a sandwich.

This idea could work for any number of products that offer the child an opportunity to make a difference in the life of a needy child in the developing world. The company could eventually produce an entire line of "Kids Helping Kids" products marketed with the message that a portion of each purchase goes to the partner's efforts. Parents will like knowing that the purchase helps make a difference for good in the world.

Family

Idea 63

Organization: Nonprofit Resource Center for Families in Crisis
Subject Area: Family – Parenting
Keyword Search: family crisis, family services, seniors

Strategy
Create innovative programs that the organization pioneers, offering partnerships in family support and crisis prevention to three primary "audiences" or markets: families, corporations and organizations, and professionals in human services or other care-giving occupations.

Underlying Value
Life does not come with an instructional manual. People often face challenges that require more support and information than they currently have.

The center can build healthier families through initiatives that also expand its sources of revenue.

Components

The center could create a series of booklets to address stressful family situations for the targeted audiences. Both booklets could be pre-sold to corporations as premium items. The corporations would distribute them to parent and teacher groups and family support groups. They could also be used as premium items for other nonprofit organizations or Family Tree memberships. Another option would be to sell them through wholesale and retail distribution networks.

Execution

Being There. This handbook for families with teens would describe family service resources (hotlines, family counseling services, drug and alcohol programs, suicide prevention resources and other crisis management aids). It would include a checklist and discussion of "danger signs" to look for during a teen's development. The checklist would cover, for example:

- Normal changes during adolescence
- How to deal with depression
- Teen stress
- Peer pressure.

This basic guide would help parents provide their teen with a supportive environment and prevent undue stress during a time of extreme change and growth.

Safe for Seniors. This handbook would provide help to seniors and families of seniors who are looking to provide a safe, supportive living environment. It could feature a detailed look at nursing and retirement homes, senior housing complexes and planned communities. Safe for Seniors would also provide a checklist of usual senior needs–physical, financial and psychological–and ask questions that are often overlooked during a search for senior housing environments and nursing homes.

In addition, the handbook would cover issues of dependence, independence, finance and "style." Its guidelines could provide the senior and his or her family an honest, "no guilt" assessment of their ability to live together in an extended family environment.

Idea 64

Organization: Nonprofit Resource Center for Families in Crisis
Subject Area: Family – Parenting
Keyword Search: crisis intervention, resource centers, human services

Strategy

Pioneer innovative programs that offer partnerships in family support and crisis prevention to three primary "audiences" or markets: families, corporations and organizations, and professionals in human services or other caregiving occupations.

Underlying Value

The organization has, through its umbrella, wide access to various groupings of markets. Tapping into this network to create sustaining initiatives will serve both the organization's mission of helping families in crisis and the goal of creating a new revenue stream.

Components

Intervention Center Franchises. This organization has already successfully operated a crisis intervention center in the city. The initiative would extend this service to a wider audience and place it in a shopping mall.

Execution

Mall Crisis Centers. The organization would provide the model and structure of the centers for national "franchising" to other human service agencies. The centers would provide their services in malls, a familiar, non-threatening environment which teens enjoy. The centers' services could include support and resources for teens and families in crisis: support for and information on increased family interaction; information on how to access and use counseling services; suicide prevention hotlines; a link to "safe houses;" and other similar services.

Also, various human service organizations could contract with the managing organization to rent space in the Mall Crisis Center. Their specialized services for teens and families might include education and counseling on issues such as suicide prevention hotlines, battered women shelters, parent support groups and other support programs.

> **Idea 65**
> **Organization:** Nonprofit Resource Center for Families Experiencing Crisis
> **Subject Area:** Family – Parenting
> **Keyword Search:** crisis prevention, employee assistance programs, human services, counseling

Strategy

Create innovative programs that the organization pioneers, offering partnerships in family support and crisis prevention to three primary "audiences" or markets: families, corporations and organizations, and professionals in human services or other care-giving occupations.

Underlying Value

Employers often see the fallout from families in crisis. An employee under tremendous stress is more prone to absenteeism and poor attention to his or her work. Corporations look to organizations like the crisis center to help them extend services to employees during the rough times.

Components

Employer Awareness Programs. An ongoing program of in-services would equip managers and personnel officers with the skills they need to recognize when an employee is under extreme stress and offer support to him or her. Training topics could include the impact of work-related stress on the family; alternative structures in stress-filled environments; alcohol and substance abuse in the workplace; and the addictive personality. These in-services would provide employers with a framework for supporting employees and their families in times of stress. The employer would benefit by helping the employee remain healthy and productive in the workplace.

Environmental Stress Audit. As part of the package, the organization would offer employers an environmental stress audit, evaluating and pinpointing the effects of stress on the employees and their families and on overall productivity. The center would be paid to administer the employer or employee stress audit or the company could administer the audit itself. If self-administered, the center would be paid to interpret, review and construct stress reduction strategies and programs.

Employee Seminar Series. As part of the stress audit, the center would customize an employer awareness training and employee topic-specific seminar series that is best suited to the stress point found during the audit. Potential seminars or training sessions for employees and their families could include:

- Self-esteem
- Combination drug use
- Dealing with grief and depression
- Forming a step (blended) family
- Teen stress and warning signs for possible suicide
- Drunk driving
- Credit card management
- Scheduling children's activities to minimize stress
- Senior abuse
- Living with one's family in retirement
- The cycle of domestic violence
- Resources for families.

The organization would identify and package topics for presentation and training that are most pertinent to employer and employee needs.

Execution

Employer Awareness Programs. Sold to corporations as a package, in-services would also include seminar programs for employees that help them identify and deal with family stresses before the point of crisis is reached.

The corporate partner might choose to buy a package of ongoing programs along with the initial stress audit and timely "check-up" audits. Or, they might choose to buy the package without the audit. Still others would only be interested in purchasing specific seminars or training sessions. The more flexible and customized the packaging, and the greater the variety of price points, the more likely it is that a corporation or organization will buy the service.

> **Idea 66**
>
> **Organization:** Nonprofit Resource Center for Families in Crisis
> **Subject Area:** Family – Parenting
> **Keyword Search:** family, crisis prevention, family membership program

Strategy

Create innovative programs that the organization pioneers, offering partnerships in family support and crisis prevention to three primary "audiences" or markets: families, corporations and organizations, and professionals in human services or other care-giving occupations.

Underlying Value

A partnership-based membership program can address the needs of two distinct markets:

- The potential donor who wants to be supportive of the organization's programs but lacks a "traditional nonprofit" vehicle for giving. (Some "donors," especially companies, can purchase a membership and justify it from a budget line rather than make a charitable donation.)
- The potential member interested in benefiting from the various services offered through the organization.

"Value added" discount arrangements and premium items are a no-cost or low-cost way to increase the perceived value of a membership program.

Components

Membership Programs. The organization would offer memberships with a choice of the "basic" or "basic with add-ons" format in order to offer varied price points to the special interest clientele. Basic memberships would feature the organization newsletter, "first mailing" invitations to special events, "first choice" volunteer opportunities, the organization's premium publications, and a family discount coupon book. The add-ons membership would feature all of those in addition to a ten to fifteen percent discount on the organization's programs, professional services and any additional products that the organization may have published.

Execution

Membership Programs. The resource center would enter into joint promotion agreements with a number of partners, such as family counselors, financial planning professionals, high school, semi-pro or professional sporting event promoters, and sporting goods retailers. Together, they would offer discounts on their products and services to the organization's members.

Idea 67

Organization: Nonprofit Resource Center for Families in Crisis
Subject Area: Family – Parenting
Keyword Search: kids, family resource, teen employment, incentive program, police

---

Strategy

Create innovative programs that the organization pioneers, offering partnerships in family support and crisis prevention to three primary "audiences" or markets: families, corporations and organizations, and professionals in human services or other care-giving occupations.

Underlying Value

This initiative distinguishes the organization from others of its kind by putting teenagers to work providing family-oriented service. The organization would serve as a primary resource for the teenage volunteer who wishes to play a major and positive role in the community. The organization's programs and services would guide and support the teens in reaching beyond themselves to help others.

Components

The center would offer programs that carry out its mission. They would differ from typical marketing projects because they do not have large income potential. Therefore, they may require underwriting.

Execution

Kids on Kids. Teenagers and youth groups often benefit from the shared stories of persons in their peer group who have experienced and emerged from stress and crisis situations. This youth speaker and peer education program would serve as a resource for youth experiencing family stress, depression, school- and peer-related stress, the changes of growing up, domestic violence, grief and other issues.

As an extension of the Kids on Kids program, the organization would develop a professional, high quality training and entertainment troupe. The group would perform skits and puppet shows on issues such as affection, safety, self-esteem and friendship at day care centers, preschools and elementary schools. The overall intent would be to begin educating children at the youngest level possible about personal pride; self esteem; safety; the rights and needs of other individuals; and the value of demonstrating care and concern for another person's well-being.

Earn It! This joint program with local police departments and justice programs would enable teens and other individuals (such as clients of battered women shelters) to work in police or justice department community service programs. Their work on a community clean-up crew or other project would earn them "credits" for hours worked. Credits could then be turned in for police end-of-the-year auction items such as bicycles, radios, VCRs, televisions and automobiles.

This is a perfect program for teens without the skills or experience required by other employers to acquire a job history, skills and responsibilities. Unemployed workers, seniors or clients from battered women shelters who need some experience in order to enter or re-enter the workforce could also be a part of the program. Earn It! provides a first step towards self-reliance and self-esteem.

Idea 68

Organization: Nonprofit Resource Center for Families in Crisis
Subject Area: Family – Parenting
Keyword Search: family resources, award program, family stress, pride, teens, neighborhood involvement

---

Strategy

Create innovative programs that the organization pioneers, offering partnerships in family support and crisis prevention to three primary "audiences" or markets:

families, corporations and organizations, and professionals in human services or other care-giving occupations.

Underlying Value
The organization is the best resource for bridging the gap that exists between families in the community who are in crisis and "healthy" families. This bridging requires a shift away from a pure "treatment" approach to one that promotes healthy, growing family environments. The main objective is to use current resources and areas of expertise to support healthy families.

Components
The center could create several awards honoring the efforts of families to improve and promote community service, pride and dignity.

Execution
Self-Esteem Awards. These awards would both honor teenagers and families and celebrate pride and dignity. Winners would be teens and their families who have survived the stress of some family hardship or crisis with unusual strength and dignity, and who serve as examples to other individuals and families facing similar situations.

Family Neighborhood Award. This annual award would celebrate the importance of strong neighborhoods as a family resource. The award would go to the neighborhood with a Neighborhood Watch program that not only prevents crime but also involves individuals and families in "watching out" for their neighbors. The organization would promote the idea that the community is partly responsible for the well being and quality of life of families. The award could be presented at an annual event, perhaps co-sponsored by a local chapter of the National Crime Prevention Council.

The Family Award. This award would be given to a family or organization that has shown consistent involvement in community awareness and service programs that promote family-related issues. Variations of this award could focus on different family members, such a teen who serves the community's families, or a senior and other adults who work to promote intergenerational awareness and cooperation. The award could also go to parents who have "survived" a family crisis and ended up building a more cooperative family environment.

132 / Cold Cash for Warm Hearts

The Corporate Family Award. This award would honor corporations that provide innovative services for working families such as latch key programs, corporate day care centers, parental leave and abuse awareness programs. The center could provide these corporate partners with a framework for providing supportive services to families. It would also illustrate the importance of the business community in promoting family growth and crisis prevention.

Idea 69

Organization: Nonprofit Resource Center for Families in Crisis
Subject Area: Family – Parenting
Keyword Search: kids, family resource, teen employment, incentive program, police

---

Strategy

Become known as the champion of families and position the department store as the recognized advocate of the values that all healthy families share. The store would also promote those aspects of society that create and support vital and successful families as a means to a better future for all.

Underlying Value

Parents are the true heroes of our society. A parenting support network can encourage this heroism. The network would offer products and services that do three things: help a parent build effective communication skills, promote high quality early childhood development, and bring practical services to busy families.

Components

The Parenting Desk. This initiative would capitalize on in-store space by creating a parenting desk in a strategic location of any store. This counter could be designated as "the place to go for tips on raising healthy and happy families." At the parenting desk, parents and guardians could ask a department store clerk about a common challenge, like getting kids to eat new foods or setting limits on behavior. The clerk would then refer the parent to a particular product or service, allowing him or her to gain access to professionally developed strategies, while communicating that "the department store is here to help solve problems."

The Sibling Celebration. This inexpensive package would offer encouragement and learning opportunities to children who have a new brother or sister. It would also help children who are in the throes of natural rivalries at home. This branded packet would include markers and a coloring book of common sibling situations along with ideas for both parents and children on how to best handle them.

The packet could also include an audio recording with child-friendly voices talking and singing about the feelings associated with being a sibling. A version for older children would foster dialogue between warring brothers and sisters. Guidelines for building good family communication and encouraging respect among siblings of any age would round out the package.

Allowance Kit. The store would partner with a nonprofit organization to market this interactive kit, which teaches money management and comes complete with stickers, games, puzzles and quizzes. As the distributor of the kit, the department store would benefit from product sales and improve its positioning as the company best prepared to help kids learn responsibility.

Treat Seats. In partnership with entertainment providers, the department store can become the resource for great prices on tickets to family events throughout the community. The store would then be associated with special family shows, such as ice skating exhibitions, musical children's plays or the circus. The goal is to act as a clearinghouse, with no requirement to actually purchase tickets. Children will get excited about the entertaining experiences associated with the department store, and parents will be pleased to save money.

Execution

The Focus on Families Trust. A trust that carries the name of the department store could communicate the marketing goals while providing a charitable funding structure. This would leverage the dual bottom line, impacting both business and social concerns.

The trust should state its mission in print advertising for the program. This could include a statement like: "This program is funded in part by the Store X Focus on Families Trust, which is dedicated to supporting and strengthening today's families and finding solutions to the issues they face."

As customers learn that the purchase of certain products will trigger a donation by the Store X Focus on Families Trust, they become more motivated to buy. Employees are also encouraged by the same incentive to sell more aggressively and to appreciate the good works undertaken by the company. In addition, they recognize incentives to perform volunteer work themselves. Furthermore, suppliers recognize the added value of a donation trigger in the purchase of their products. Since they are also exposed to the message of the trust, the Focus on Families dimension will have an impact on the employees of all these businesses as well.

Idea 70

Organization: Private Packaged Goods Company
Subject Area: Family – Volunteerism
Keyword Search: family, family service, volunteer, service vacations, public schools

Strategy
Focus on helping to create and sustain strong and cohesive families. Achieving this will involve targeting a consumer who also works to sustain a healthy and happy younger generation.

Underlying Value
This initiative communicates the message that the company is concerned about children and families. It also positions the company as one that cares about the purchaser–the parent or guardian shopping for his or her family.

Components
Family Service Adventures. The family that serves together not only stays together but thrives with a sense of moral purpose and valuable shared experience. To communicate that this packaged goods company is concerned about children and families, the initiative would illustrate how families can serve their community. It would then offer practical ways for families to answer the call to action.

The Important Role of Schools. The company should take special pride in fostering service initiatives that benefit schools. A prime example would be a project that tracks the hours a family spends in service to the school. The company would participate by providing tally sheets to school administrators. Then, when certain hourly targets are met, the company would make a cash donation to the school.

This school-sanctioned, "close-to-home" initiative would offer families with children a special incentive to participate in the company's public purpose effort. Schools could also be motivated to promote the initiative. They would gain double the benefits by setting up convenient projects such as seasonal cleanups and landscaping efforts to garner "points" toward the goal of a cash gift or other donation.

Execution

Make a Difference Day. The company could kick off its Family Service Adventures concept with a promotion that provides many ways for consumers to participate easily. For example, a toll-free number could be set up to match families with local projects.

Product features, print and television advertising, and in-store promotions would all be used for the promotion. Packaging would offer discount coupons to consumers who buy the product and have their coupon stamped at a Make a Difference Day service location. Celebrity spokespersons could make public appearances or appear in print or radio ads. These public figures could be paired with motivational messages on the importance of families in service. They could also tell the stories of families who have reaped benefits, both personal and social, from their service adventures.

National Service Summit. An attractive variation on Make a Difference Day would be a company-sponsored National Service Summit. This convention would be modeled directly on the first United States Citizen Service Summit that took place in 1997. The meeting received broad exposure in the United States, where it was directly promoted by President Bill Clinton and several other high-ranking officials. These leaders all expressed their belief that average citizens must work together to address social problems. The company would present a similar concept, involving participants in dialogue about a new strategy for community service and leadership. High-ranking public servants and leaders from various disciplines could be invited to speak at the event or endorse it.

Idea 71

Organization: Manufacturer of Liquid Goods
Subject Area: Family – Volunteerism
Keyword Search: family, service projects, volunteer, packaged goods manufacturer

Strategy

As a manufacturer, this company rarely "touches" the end consumer. This public purpose marketing strategy is designed to reach beyond the manufacturer and food retailer to communicate directly with the end consumer.

Underlying Value

Even though it is the liquid food manufacturer who actually buys the processing, packaging and distribution systems, it is the average consumer who can greatly influence–through his or her pressure on supermarkets–decisions about using and tangibly identifying the company's packaging. In essence, the public buys companies, not products. The company will offer consumers an opportunity to feel that they are involved and their participation matters.

Components

The company can become the nationally known expert on helping families make a positive difference in their community and their country. In addition to helping consumers express their desire to serve, the company would recruit groups that have worthwhile work for volunteer families to perform. Nonprofit organizations that understand the constraints of working with volunteers of different ages and abilities make excellent candidates.

Execution

The programs could be organized in a variety of ways, including:
- Half-day to multiple-day activities that families sign up for as an enhancement of a current holiday
- Half-day to multiple-day service activities scheduled into a vacation package
- Local opportunities that are perfect for three-day weekends and other leisure times that families spend close to home

♦ One- to two-week service vacations that comprehensively integrate both relaxation and service to others.

Packaging. Liquid food packaging offers a handy mechanism for promoting the company's program. Working in partnership with manufacturers, the company could attach discount coupons or tokens for "Company X Family Service Adventures" to product packages. Images on cardboard backing could illustrate and tell brief stories of families serving their communities.

Donation Triggers. Advertising and shelf talkers would send the message to consumers that their purchase of an item produced with the company packaging will allow a percentage of the price to help fund these service opportunities.

Company X Family Reunions. These reunions would give the company access to their customers' relatives and potential product buyers. The company would provide discounted teleconferencing services to facilitate communication between family members who live far from one another. This pay-for-use service would be available by calling a toll-free telephone number. The service would also promote extended family participation in service holidays. Success stories of families reunited in service would provide excellent promotional material.

Idea 72

Organization: Telecommunications Provider
Subject Area: Family – Work-Life Balance
Keyword Search: family, balance, working families, technology, telecommunications

Strategy

Become known as the country's premier proponent of innovative employee programs that help families balance work and home responsibilities.

Underlying Value

Modern life is hectic and stressful, especially for families. Often, both parents hold full-time jobs and must meet the challenge of providing their children with adequate care during the day or supervision after school. In addition, an unprecedented number of teenage or single parents are facing special parenting challenges.

The telecommunications company cares about these current issues. Companies like this one lose millions of dollars each year through low productivity due to worker anxiety, disruptions, and time lost because of inadequate or inappropriate child care. The company can define this challenge and lead the way to cost-effective programs. These services would measurably help families balance work and home in addition to improving productivity figures for businesses.

Components

"Check-In" Strategies. A common concern among working parents is supervision for their children after school ends and before a parent arrives at home. Parents would like to have their children call to check in after school, but often children do not have time before after-school activities begin, nor do they have access to a phone.

The company could market a "Check-in Package" that would include a cell phone, a pager and a special use option requiring a code to activate the service with cellular phone calls limited to only a few numbers. Parents would be able to page their children and tell them to call Mom or Dad at work. Children would be able to dial their personal code, then an authorized phone number, most likely their parent's work number.

Unfortunately, children have a tendency to encounter mishaps from time to time. A "Check-in Cell Phone" could be invaluable to children for summoning help and letting parents know where they are. Phones might include a position location device to aid emergency personnel in finding the child in the event that he or she is alone and unable to describe his or her exact location.

The Check-in Package would provide parents with added peace of mind and instant communication with their children. This valuable tool would help teach children how the telephone can help them become more responsible and caring. As the first to offer such a package, the company could attract working parents as new customers. The company would donate a percentage of all sales to a fund that helps low-income parents obtain Check-in Packages for their children.

Execution

Wrist Phones. Technology for wrist phones is here, and these products will soon become more widely available. The company could introduce them to the public by making them part of a Check-in Package for children of working parents. The wrist phone would lend additional peace of mind to employees who have an elderly or disabled relative at home, or have concern for another person who has health problems. The person would always have access to a phone in case of an emergency. A percentage of profits from wrist phone sales could be donated to charity.

Health and Wellness

Idea 73

Organization: Cancer Relief Organization and Fortune 500 Car Manufacturer
Subject Area: Health and Wellness – Chronic Illness
Keyword Search: cancer, car, automobile, fund, safety, security systems

Strategy
Through financial and service-based initiatives, support cancer relief efforts using the company's financial and human resources.

Underlying Value
A partnership with a cancer relief organization can communicate that this company is a leader in the spirit of customer service. It can also powerfully intensify the company's reputation for excellent corporate citizenship. As a leading manufacturer of automobiles, the company has consistently linked its commitment

to quality with product safety. This initiative extends that connection to include the corporation's concern for personal safety.

Components
The Safeguard Initiative. An automobile safeguard system is already a popular product for new customers. It provides the company with a dramatic opportunity to demonstrate its commitment to an organization that profoundly impacts a sense of personal security for millions of families every year. In a sense, the cancer relief organization serves as a safeguard to citizens just as an electronic engine immobilizer serves as a safeguard in a car. Both provide customers with comfort in the knowledge that someone is watching out for them.

Execution
Travel Security Systems. The company could offer several individual or branded sets of products in partnership with the cancer relief organization. Each product would address family safety in general or food safety in particular for customers traveling by automobile. These could include a sanitary travel pillow, a natural fiber blanket that can be stored in the trunk, a first aid kit designed by the organization's nurses and other products. Purchasing a set or an individual product would prompt a donation by the company to the cancer organization.

Idea 74

Organization: Cancer Relief Fund and Fortune 500 Car Manufacturer
Subject Area: Health and Wellness – Chronic Illness
Keyword Search: cancer, covenant, credit card

Strategy
Create financial and service-oriented initiatives to support cancer relief efforts using the company's financial and human resources.

Underlying Value
Excellent health care can mean the difference between life and death for a person who has been diagnosed with cancer. Partnering with a cancer relief fund

serves to communicate to the public that the company embodies a spirit of customer service. It also intensifies the company's reputation for excellence in corporate citizenship.

Components

Cancer Relief Funding Covenant. This covenant, which capitalizes on the company's known reputation for commitment, could be named jointly for the company and the cancer relief fund. It states that the purchase of this manufacturer's products or services brings with it a promise to provide excellence. Choosing this company over its competitors would directly benefit the partnering organization, which demonstrates commitment to excellence.

Execution

The Customer Covenant. This agreement, signed during a car purchase, could round up the cost of the automobile to a specific figure. The balance from the sale price would then be dedicated to the cancer relief fund. At the time of purchase, an individual could also promise that, when the time comes to trade in the automobile, he or she would offer a percentage of that sale to the fund. The car dealer would calculate this tax-deductible donation on the customer's behalf.

The Corporate Covenant. This program would mirror the customer covenant. It would tie fleet purchases or lease arrangements to donations for the cancer fund's programs. The covenant could take the form of a partnership that includes the fleet manager's employees. The employees would get to see their business use of a company automobile make a positive difference for their families and neighbors who struggle with cancer. Fleet owners might even have the covenant imprinted on their company cars. For example, "Company X is proud to partner with Nonprofit Y to support cancer nurses in this community."

The Credit Card Covenant. The company could partner with a bank to offer customers a credit card that triggers a discount on the purchase of a car. As an added incentive, the card could feature a financial bonus to the car buyer. If a customer uses the card to make a donation to the cancer fund, the company would double the amount of his or her car purchase rebate. The bank would send a message about "investing" in the future of individuals in the community.

Idea 75

Organization: Cancer Relief Organization and Fortune 500 Car Manufacturer
Subject Area: Health and Wellness – Chronic Illness
Keyword Search: cancer, car, telephone card, rebate program

Strategy

Through financial and service-based initiatives, support cancer relief efforts using the company's financial and human resources.

Underlying Value

A partnership with a cancer relief organization can communicate that this company is a leader in the spirit of customer service. It can also powerfully intensify the company's reputation for excellent corporate citizenship.

Components

Customer Involvement Initiative. This initiative could announce to the public that everyone benefits from supporting the cancer relief fund. The company would remind customers that it feels good to make a difference. The marketing under this initiative would encourage consumers to purchase an automobile, accessories or replacements parts that will benefit them while also stimulating a company donation to the cancer organization and its valuable programs. Having their auto serviced at a company shop would also link them to a positive difference for their families and neighbors who struggle with cancer. Packaging of company products and signage in the waiting area of the service centers could promote this initiative.

Execution

Cancer Relief Telephone Card. Many prepaid long distance cards are marketed with the message that a percentage of the purchase price will go to a charitable cause. The car manufacturer and cancer relief organization could intensify the value of their long distance card. Not only would a portion of the proceeds go to the cancer organization, but using the card would also earn the consumer points toward a rebate on his or her next car purchase.

> **Idea 76**
>
> **Organization:** Company and Nonprofit Cancer Relief Organization
> **Subject Area:** Health and Wellness – Chronic Illness
> **Keyword Search:** cancer, survival, celebration, life

Strategy
Create a partnership to become the nation's leader in cause-corporate support for cancer relief efforts.

Underlying Value
A public purpose marketing program will help position the private company and nonprofit organization as the nation's experts in the celebration of life.

Components
Celebrating the Gifts of Life Initiative. Although this nonprofit partner helps people in a time of need, it is not characterized by a sense of tragedy. Even among the most critically ill patients, the care providers can bring to their work a positive attitude and a strong belief that good can come from any situation. These care providers personify the celebration of life theme even when their contributions seem small or momentarily overshadowed by the intensity of the disease process. The company could incorporate this theme across its divisions or subsidiaries, offering a variety of products and services.

Execution
Remember Me Theme. Memorializing cancer patients is one way to celebrate the everyday victories of life. It provides an appropriate, caring way for the company to communicate: "All of us are in this life together. Let's make the best of it."

The Winners Wall. As a leisure retailer, the company is familiar with public displays of recognition. For instance, the winners of a local sporting event will often appear on the wall of a restaurant or bar. This company has a unique opportunity to enhance this idea by adding photographs of local citizens who, with the support of the nonprofit, have overcome cancer. The photos could even show the former patient in celebratory poses alongside his or her former care provider. The goal would be for the customer to ask, "Who is that?" When they lean closer to look, they could read about the company's role in celebrating these victories and its commitment to the organization's valuable services.

Celebrating Surviving Cancer Book. Statistically speaking, every family can expect to be touched by cancer at some point. This book would feature testimonials from cancer survivors, their families and their care providers. It would include suggestions for healthy lifestyle habits, stress relief and cancer screening tests, including where to get tested. It could also emphasize that experiencing cancer is not the end of life. In fact, for most people, the experience reinforces the belief that every day is special and should be cherished.

Idea 77

Organization: Nonprofit Cancer Relief Organization
Subject Area: Health and Wellness – Chronic Illness
Keyword Search: cancer, investing in others, character, cancer patient, compassion

Strategy
Create a public purpose marketing program that will position the company and the cancer relief organization as the national experts in the celebration of life.

Underlying Value
Most people in our society are very concerned about character, integrity and moral decline. The care providers in this nonprofit organization offer people a dramatic reprieve from the apathy and selfishness paraded through the media that supposedly reflect our current moral state. These care providers are role models in the finest sense–people of compassion and dedication who work hard to make the world a better place.

This initiative offers both partners an opportunity to communicate the abundance of good in individuals while celebrating the quality of collective moral strength. The theme of "Celebrating the Quality of Our Character" also serves to raise awareness of exceptional organizations like this company. The company can dramatize this theme throughout its family of companies, offering products and services that relate to two dimensions of character that care providers demonstrate: virtue in action and investing in others.

Components

Virtue in Action. To some extent, each of us is cautious about our complex, sometimes dangerous world. It is difficult to overlook our own fears or hurtful experiences to step forward and help someone in need. We are attracted to virtuous behavior but often need small opportunities to help someone else, choices for compassion upon which we can build a stronger foundation of caring.

Investing In Others. Many people do not act on their highest principles because they believe it will require too much effort. The "investing in others" initiative could offer credit for service. The customer would receive tangible dividends for fulfilling a promise to help someone in need–a cancer patient. The company would serve as a model, demonstrating how people who serve others enjoy more fulfilling lives. Consumers could be encouraged to engage in acts of compassion simply by making normal, everyday purchases.

Execution

Pence Parade. This "Virtue in Action" promotion would invite customers of the company businesses to give the pennies presently in their pockets to help the nonprofit cancer relief organization. Instead of emphasizing the pittance such a donation would represent, the company would celebrate the Pence Parade by offering discounts on drinks or future hotel stays to anyone who participates. This initiative is similar to one that is used successfully by a prominent disease relief organization. Thousands of people save pennies for months leading up to the organization's annual telethon, expecting to make that donation every year.

Frequent Purchaser Program. This initiative would enable a person to demonstrate the quality of investing in others. Every time a consumer purchases a product or visits a company location, he or she would receive a frequent purchaser card at no cost. For every tenth purchase or stay, for example, the customer would receive an eleventh product free and stimulate a donation to the nonprofit. When the patron redeems this earned benefit, he or she would also receive a card, brochure or newsletter that reports recent enhancements of the nonprofit service. Or, the promotional piece could tell a heartwarming story of how support for the organization made a difference to one cancer patient.

148 / Cold Cash for Warm Hearts

Idea 78

Organization: Home Care Nurses Association
Subject Area: Health and Wellness – Community
Keyword Search: nurse, caregiver, home safety, healthy

Strategy

Leverage the perceptions most Americans have that nurses are generally compassionate experts in care-giving and that visiting nurses in particular are trustworthy and sensitive to issues of cost and convenience. With this strategy, the association will achieve:

- A stronger, more loyal relationship with its corporate partners, their customers, employees and the general public
- A broad range of products associated with the organization
- An enhanced reputation for the association and its marketing partners
- A diversified income-generation program.

Underlying Value

Family Preparedness. This theme is based on the association's work in home health care. It advocates health, safety and security, as well as readiness for emergencies with the kinds of products and services that a visiting nurse would recommend. Every family needs a supply of products "just in case." They also need training in certain skills for those unexpected situations. Nurses are well positioned as advocates of preventative care; they are people who notice what might go wrong and recommend ways to avoid painful, if not tragic, consequences.

Components

Safety Comes First. Who better than a nurse to deal with the day-to-day issues of family safety? Each initiative under Safety Comes First addresses questions that visiting nurses are asked on a regular basis.

Screening Saves Lives. Most of us hear a lot about health screening, especially through public service announcements that encourage us to be tested for problems for which we might be at risk. The real issue for most Americans, though, is connecting personal risk with adequate motivation to actually get the screening done. The association can help make health screening a much more common part of family life.

Execution

The Family Health IQ Test. This simple product could be available for purchase in any pharmacy, supermarket or convenience store. It could also be sold in conjunction with a comprehensive publicity campaign on family health readiness. The campaign would ask the consumer: Does your family really know how to stay healthy? Do you know the warning signs of common diseases? Is medicine in your home safe from children and pets? Nurses are trusted to know the answers to these and many other questions. Americans could be encouraged to set aside one day a year to sit down with their families, take a "health IQ test" and learn simple and inexpensive ways to make their lives safer and healthier.

Incentive Programs. Most people remember the promise of a lollipop after a childhood booster shot. Nurses know that incentives work for both children and adults. Association nurses could be encouraged to contribute creative ideas for motivating people to get certain tests. Such ideas might include the following.

- Women could receive flower or vegetable garden seeds and a discount coupon on a mammogram under the theme of staying healthy for another season.
- Consumers who recycle reading glasses at a local pharmacy could receive a discount on their next flu shot.
- A plush toy could be offered as a reward for a child who has received the full set of recommended vaccinations.
- Licensed drivers could receive discount coupons for an oil change, tune-up or other car maintenance for having their vision tested
- The association could coordinate the receipt of free or discounted access to a pay-per-view sports event on cable television for men who are screened for prostate cancer.
- Lotions high in sun protection factor (SPF) could be offered to customers who are screened for vulnerability to skin cancer.

The more creative the incentives are, the broader the potential consumer appeal would be.

Idea 79

Organization: Home Care Nurses Association
Subject Area: Health and Wellness – Community
Keyword Search: healthy, caregiver, nurses, corporate health initiatives, employee benefits

Strategy

Leverage the perception most people have that nurses are generally compassionate experts in care-giving. Reinstate the idea that visiting nurses in particular are trustworthy and sensitive to issues of cost and convenience. With this strategy, the association may achieve the following:

- A stronger, more loyal relationship with its corporate partners, their customers, employees and the public
- A broad range of products associated with the organization
- An enhanced reputation for the association and its marketing partners
- A diversified income-generation program.

Underlying Value

Better than anyone, nurses can communicate to individuals the rewards of good health, and are well positioned to offer us effective incentives to pursue healthier lifestyles. And, most visiting nurses enjoy the chance to celebrate good health. An initiative called "The Rewards of Healthy Living Initiative: Incentives for Success" would build on the perception of nurses as compassionate and caring. It would also reflect a person's willingness to allow a nurse to teach and lead him or her toward healthier living when the motivation to get there alone is missing.

Components

Celebrating a Healthy America. Many organizations have annual events, such as a sanctioned day or week, when they seek to call national attention to their particular cause. Celebrating a Healthy America would be a set of products, regularly updated and consistently promoted, that would help institutionalize concern for good health as part of each person's daily life.

Living Well: A Service to Corporations and Their Employees. This service would promote and reward wellness choices. It would be based on a set of achievable milestones, and would celebrate even the most modest accom-

Health and Wellness / 151

plishments. The nurses association could manage the Living Well program or it could simply set up programs that are tailored to individual workplaces.

Execution

Health Passport. These passports, celebrating a healthy nation, could be for both adults and children. Designed to look like a real passport, they would include stamps from countries around the world. A tasty and healthy native recipe would accompany each country's stamp, along with an explanation of how people there enjoy exercise. The passport could include passes to health clubs, seminars on healthy living, and coupons for discounts on a wide variety of health-related products.

Purchase of the passport would not only promote education for the person using it, but also educate him or her about the association and how it makes a difference in local communities. In addition, each purchase would trigger a donation to the local affiliate association.

Incentives and Rewards for Exercise. This service to companies and their employees would feature a point system for physical activities–anything from jogging, karate and yoga to thirty minutes on a stair-stepping machine. Participants would tally their points and redeem them at the end of each month for rewards as simple as a T-shirt or fanny pack, or as valuable as a fitness assessment by a nurse or a contribution to the employee's favorite charity. A personalized wellness program, a fitness encyclopedia, theater passes, or tickets to a sporting event could also be rewards.

Idea 80

Organization: Emergency Response and Community Health Service Provider
Subject Area: Health and Wellness – Community
Keyword Search: health, safety, emergency, community health

Strategy

Increase income generation potential by expanding the perception of the service beyond just emergency response. Also, position the organization as the national expert in community health and safety.

Underlying Value

"The Hometown Action Network Initiative" is designed to reposition the service provider as the agent for bringing health and safety to communities across the region. It reminds the public that the health service provider exists to bring meaningful actions to hometowns large or small. This team of professionals wants the best for people, regardless of their geographic or economic circumstances. They will come to any location to provide exceptional health care, health and safety education, and encouragement. When other expertise is needed, they foster a network of community health professionals, arranging for the prompt arrival of supplemental care.

The Living Well Covenant. While health and safety emergencies happen in a variety of circumstances, the vast majority of rescues carried out by any air ambulance are related to automobile accidents, hiking and climbing or small aircraft crashes. Here is an opportunity for businesses that profit from these activities to focus on the flip side of their relationship with the service. They can help the service provider to promote preventative health care and quality lifestyle choices.

Automobile and airplane manufacturers, auto and aviation fuel producers and distributors, and resorts and wilderness equipment retailers would engage in a covenant to self-impose a tax on their products. This tax money would go directly to the health care service to fund Living Well programs in local communities.

Execution

Automatic Teller Machine (ATM) Rebates. These electronic boxes have become a staple of the modern lifestyle, even when a customer is charged for making the transaction. A banking partner could program its ATM machines so that consumers can make a donation to the service provider simply by pressing a button. Clearly posted instructions would note that for every donation deducted from the consumer's savings or checking account, he or she will receive a rebate on ATM charges. Rebates would be indicated on each month's statement. Besides prompting the consumer to reason: "At least I'm doing some good," the rebates can, in fact, trigger increased usage of the ATM. Banking partners would still make a profit from the transaction, but would be further positioned as willing to make a sacrifice in order to support the health and safety issues their customers care about.

Idea 81

Organization: Community Mental Health Provider
Subject Area: Health and Wellness – Community
Keyword Search: mental health, community health, stress management

Strategy
Develop a new vision that will enable the community mental health provider to surpass the competition, earn additional income, generate excitement, and improve its image both internally and externally.

Underlying Value
These mechanisms would be designed to promote the organization's new care standards, mobility, accessibility, and emphasis on dignity and staying well. Some would be targeted to middle-income users, some to low-income, and some to both. Services should be ongoing, sustainable programs that earn income above their costs.

Components
Pre-sell strategy. To reduce expenses and financial risk, these products and services should be pre-sold to corporations. Before they are developed, businesses could pre-order them in bulk for distribution to their own clients. In this way, the organization can avoid spending its own money to develop products and services, and will never be in the position of having a product with no market.

Execution
Family and Friends Care. The mental health provider could show its clients that it cares about their entire family by offering a joint program with one or more veterinarians. Each visit to the organization would earn a discounted visit to the vet or vice versa. As a result, the mental health provider would be teaching the value of health maintenance check-ups for animals as well as for people.

Mental Health Tune-Up. The organization could provide short-term counseling to counteract situational stress. A multitude of situations in people's lives can cause depression and stress, including holidays, divorce, death of a loved one, a new job, a major move, marriage, new stepchildren, retirement, bankruptcy, tax time, major illness, children moving away from home, children going to school for the first time, dating, and making a major purchase. The organization would package a

"Provider X Sounding Board Service" that offers three sessions of counseling to help reduce these anxieties. Some counseling might even be offered jointly with a business that can help relieve the cause of the stress. For example, it could offer tax stress counseling with H and R Block: "They prepare your taxes, we repair your mind." Counseling could be offered both at the organization and at other locations. Another service might be "We Mend Broken Hearts," counseling specifically for people ending relationships.

Corporate Teen and Employer Training. The organization could contract with fast food and retail corporations that typically employ teens. Services would include training managers in a number of skill areas, such as:
- Finding and hiring the best teenage workers
- Mentoring employees who are new to the world of work
- Understanding the emotional challenges teenagers face
- Techniques for managing this unique population
- Fun and creative incentives for teenage workers
- Training in conflict management and conflict mediation.

Roses for Moms. The provider could add dignity to the patient's birthing experience (Medicaid paying, too) by sending flowers to her home after she delivers a baby. For a fee, the provider could also offer a contract service to the mother that enables her to rent a nurse to help her at home in the first weeks of motherhood.

Idea 82

Organization: Mental Health Center
Subject Area: Health and Wellness – Mental Health
Keyword Search: mental health, emotional intelligence, consulting firm, personal improvement, personal coaching

Strategy
Increase access and acceptance of mental health care among the general population by creating a consulting business unit within a center.

Underlying Value
The center can capitalize on existing strengths, expertise and knowledge, and repackage these skills to target specific markets in need of their services.

For instance, if the center has expertise in trauma, eating disorders and ADHD, it can create products that address these problems and sell them for a fee. Target markets in need of these services include law enforcement, school systems, churches, preschools and other service-oriented organizations. Instead of offering its services free of charge, the organization can sell them to clients who are able to pay.

Components

The center may have expertise in emotional intelligence (EQ). The goal, then, is to provide personal coaching and personal improvement starting with EQ testing. In order to provide EQ-based services, the mental health center must invest in a license that enables clinicians to administer the EQ test. If this is not a viable option, it should consider other strengths within the center. Once planning is complete, the center should target area business with the following products.

EQ Test. The center would administer EQ tests to measure employees' emotional strengths and weaknesses. It would then offer personal coaching sessions with employees to review test results and set personal development goals.

EQ Profiles. The center would profile top salespersons or managers to determine what common emotional strengths exist and offer training on these specific strengths.

EQ Training Workshops. When enough data has been collected from profiling executives, the center would offer on-site EQ workshops to employees who seek self-improvement, career enhancement and success- building strategies.

Execution

Business Development. The center could establish relationships with local businesses by attending chamber of commerce and networking events. This would allow center leaders to extend business relationships that may already exist with current vendors or providers.

Complimentary Testing and Workshops. The center could offer free EQ-based products to a targeted group–chamber members, young CEOs, local government officials and other community leaders. A key to success would be to target people who are well connected and could serve as "ambassadors" for this product.

Idea 83

Organization: Service Provider for Visually Impaired Citizens
Subject Area: Health and Wellness – Disabilities
Keyword Search: visually impaired, celebration, disabilities, blind, eye products

Strategy

Create a social marketing relationship with a corporation to achieve the following results:

- Improved brand strength and market positioning, leading to a competitive advantage
- Increased sales and growth in market share leading to improved profitability
- Established loyalty for the organization as a respected corporate citizen and a valued participant in the communities where it has a presence.

Underlying Value

The "Yes Eye (I) Can: Celebrating Abilities and Eliminating Stereotypes" initiative would offer a corporate partner the unique opportunity to position itself as a national leader in efforts to challenge stereotypes about disabilities. Its impact can be so profound as to drastically reduce the presence of damaging stereotypes. The provider can present a series of products and promotions that will generate profits but, perhaps just as significantly, also help establish a strong brand identity.

Components

ID the Blind Person. This poster series would promote the fact that one cannot always tell when another person is visually impaired. Via media (including billboards), the public would be encouraged to view photographs of a group of people and pick the person they think is blind. They would then learn that every person on the poster is actually legally blind. The poster series challenges our stereotypes; the truth is the blind person usually does not look different from any other person. The same campaign could be used to challenge stereotypes about people with other kinds of disabilities.

The Sensory Olympics. An observation commonly made by persons living with a disability is that non-impaired individuals often take their senses for granted. Out of necessity, visually impaired people frequently develop a very strong sense of smell and hearing to help compensate for their lack of sight while hearing impaired people often develop hawklike vision. Persons with any number of physical challenges are often far more sensitive to touch. All such individuals cultivate a remarkable ability to learn using their non-impaired senses. This annual event would call attention to this reality and would offer tests to identify the individual with the best sense of smell, touch, taste, hearing and sight. Outcomes would likely astound the general public, who would learn about the abilities of people with impairments.

The Sensory Olympics would not only be held for individuals with an impairment. Corporate teams could be organized to go head-to-head in sensory competitions, with progressively uncommon objects and fragrances to identify. Each team would pay a fee to compete and others could pay admission to be part of the audience. As the popularity of the event grows, organizations could vie for the "Good Sense Cup," which would remain with the team as long as it continued winning. The Sensory Olympics would be a highly mediagenic event that establishes new rules about senses, promoting reliance on all our faculties to better appreciate life in all its aspects.

Execution

Eye Product Purchases. Either online or in a retail location, the organization could partner with an eyewear retailer to establish a system where each order would create a donation to the organization. Makers of contact lenses, saline solution, eye drops and sunglasses are all logical partners. Other possible participants include manufacturers of photographic film, digital cameras and equipment, or picture frames.

The "Insight" Private Label Brand. Branding is an important part of any marketing equation. The organization and its corporate partner have a significant opportunity to generate profit by selling their own brand of products. Consumers would come to look for the Insight name, a label that tells them that each purchase benefits the organization's programs. Packaging and promotional materials would also mention that visually impaired people were employed to manufacture or package the product, that instructions will be included in large type or via audio recording, and that the product has been produced in accordance with the highest standards for quality and accessibility.

Idea 84

Organization: Transportation Service for Disabled Citizens
Subject Area: Health and Wellness – Disabilities
Keyword Search: disability, transportation, handicapped, toys, community service

Strategy

Position the transportation provider as the expert in safe mobility, extending beyond disabled and handicapped consumers to educate people about handicaps and reduce stereotypes of this population.

Underlying Value

If this organization is perceived as a service for everyone, not only for the poor or physically handicapped, it will garner attention and be used by a more affluent population who can afford to pay a fee. For example, a working mother whose car is in the shop has a mobility problem when she cannot get her son to his music lesson. If this service is properly marketed with profit considerations built in, the organization can use this income to subsidize services to the poor.

Components

The service provider would offer market-specific transportation programs and safety-centered products and services in the targeted city or region. Some products and services would have national implications. Activities could include defensive driving classes, maintenance services, and ten-point safety tests that check tires, alignment, seat belts and other essential devices.

Execution

Accessible City Guidebooks. These attractive, easy-to-handle guidebooks would feature places and activities in the city or region that are accessible to older people and physically challenged individuals. The organization may want to consider large print editions, Braille editions and audio recordings. Guidebooks should include floor plans that indicate wheelchair entrances, ramps, accessible drinking fountains, phones, restrooms and elevators. Eventually, the concept could be expanded and perhaps franchised to programs in other cities, such as

YMCA's, that regularly address issues of accessibility.

A variation of American Automobile Association's TripTiks could serve as a spin-off from the guidebook. This service would custom-design travel plans for people who are wheelchair-bound or otherwise physically challenged. The maps and information package would identify accessible hotels, inns, restaurants, bathrooms, transportation services, medical services, entertainment and events along the route. This service could be created on contract with outside agencies with the organization being paid an overriding fee.

These guidebooks would be a natural match for a number of corporations—chains of hotels, motels, movie theaters, convenience stores, restaurants, vendors interested in public purpose marketing or those that want to reach affluent, physically challenged people. A major nursing home chain that wishes to be recognized for promoting active and independent residents might also be an attractive partner. Another possibility is a retirement community that wants to attract financially able but physically challenged residents.

Wooden Toy Van. The organization could create a wooden toy van, complete with fold-down ramps, wheelchair restraints and seat belts. The van could be available as a membership benefit and an item for sale to the public. This product would give consumers a low-cost connection to the organization. Fisher-Price and other toy manufacturers would be logical companies to approach for production and distribution. The toy could be pre-sold to organizations such as the Special Olympics as a moneymaker or membership benefit.

Idea 85

Organization: National Foundation for the Hearing Impaired
Subject Area: Health and Wellness – Disabilities
Keyword Search: family health, infant hearing test, child development, safety, hearing impaired, deaf

Strategy

Build on existing strengths and purposes to position the organization as the premier facilitating partner in hearing services for individuals, families, the community, corporations and the medical profession.

Underlying Value

The foundation will become known as an organization concerned with the needs of families, specifically new parents. Its direct services, educational programs and publications will feature prevention as a focal point.

Components

Families need a number of resources to be prepared for hearing-related issues, including family hearing screenings and educational seminars on the prevention and identification of ear infections, congenital hearing defects, trauma and hearing stimulation kits.

The "Promotion of the Parent as Partner: an Ally in Good Hearing and Hearing Protection" initiative would feature seminars, product development and publications.

Execution

Hearing Stimulation Kits. Designed for new parents with infants, the kit would include:
- Bells
- A rattle
- An audio recording for sound stimulation
- A "hearing milestone" developmental chart
- Membership in a toy club
- A set of "how to" cards for crib or changing table
- Methods to provide a stimulating sound environment
- Tips on keeping a baby's ears clean, identifying ear infections and teaching a child to blow his or her nose properly
- Information on the pros and cons of ear piercing.

In partnership with a toy manufacturer, the Hearing Stimulation Kit could be distributed to new parents through hospital premiums and sold at retail toy outlets. It could also become a premium item for insurance companies and child photo franchises. All items would be labeled "Brought to you by Foundation X."

Museums

Idea 86

Organization: Museum
Subject Area: Museums – Membership
Keyword Search: culture, exhibits, toys

Strategy

Promote the museum as a valuable resource for:
- High quality experiences for a broadening base of museum audiences
- Expanding the region's cultural scene
- Profound marketing opportunities for corporations and businesses.

Underlying Value

The museum will offer its corporate partner innovative and strategic marketing opportunities that meet six criteria:

- Simplicity
- Durability (momentum over time and a sense of authenticity)
- Increased profitability (with measurable results)
- Employee involvement
- Positive social change (including tangible evidence of increased enthusiasm for the museum's mission)
- Exclusivity and ownership (including a public perception that this is a very special relationship).

Components

The Museum Passport. This benefit-enhanced and market-driven membership program, like its government-issued inspiration, would provide the holder access to new worlds. The Museum Passport also symbolizes inclusion in an exclusive–although not elitist–group. The corporate partners would supply many of the privileges that come with the passport, such as discounts on restaurants, entertainment, travel services, essential services and merchandise. In addition, the passport holder could gain special status, like an ambassador. The more exclusive ambassador passport would carry special privileges and recognition.

Passport holders would enjoy discounted museum admission and special access to exhibit previews, special events and programs sponsored by corporate partners.

Execution

Customer-Engaging Products. One of the most important themes of a museum is its emphasis on experiencing design. Customer-engaging products would allow users to build, rearrange, add to and subtract from an item they have purchased. They would get to experience how their choices impact design. Manufacturers of toys, gadgets, tools, electronics, automobiles, appliances, textiles, and paper products and are all excellent candidates to partner with the museum in developing merchandise that is targeted to inventive consumers (and their parents).

Items might be designed only for fun and creative expression. Or, products could be designed for the consumer's practical use. Lamps that can be contorted into interesting positions; chairs that can be transformed into tables or beds; and storage containers that can be attached to other storage containers to create unique shapes and spaces are good examples.

Idea 87

Organization: Art Museum
Subject Area: Museums – Treasures
Keyword Search: culture, exhibits

Strategy

Position the museum as a dynamic organism and a symbol of specific values shared by the people of the community. It will also become recognized as a market-driven, financially self-sufficient organization.

Underlying Value

The museum will become known as one of the *living* treasures of the region since it represents a broad range of activities as well as artifacts. It can present dance, music, food, dress, crafts and games, among other activities. This educational atmosphere allows visitors to not only read and observe but also interact with artists. They can learn about the genesis of ideas and the lifestyles and values carried on by these agents of creativity.

Components

Under the umbrella of living treasures, the museum could pursue several themes to develop a comprehensive and well-integrated set of products and services.

Hidden Treasures. The museum would create an exhibit that highlights arts, crafts, music, dance and other cultural assets that have never been celebrated before.

Mysteries of the Region. What sometimes keeps an artifact alive is that scientists still do not understand its meaning or the complete relevance of its symbolism. This theme would focus on anthropological and artistic questions curators still face.

Sharing the Pride. The museum could bring the "living treasures" to the citizens of the community who would otherwise not be exposed to their own region's culture and heritage. This theme lends itself well to the design of enterprising activities.

Execution

Craft Carts. These rolling museum shops would be stationed in the city's airport, allowing the museum to sell products and promote museum activities to visitors who are arriving in the city.

The Museum Test Drive. The museum can offer visitors a challenge for three months: "If you stay for less than thirty minutes, your visit is free." This concept has been tested before and saw great success. Visitors pay admission and receive a time-clock card indicating the precise minute they entered the premises. As visitors tour the museum, staff is available for question-and-answer sessions and as personal guides to the exhibits. If all goes well, the visitor looks down at his watch only to find he has surpassed the thirty-minute time frame. This initiative will bring visitors to the museum. Most likely, few of them will request their money back even if they did tour in less than thirty minutes because the museum is strong in exhibits and programs.

Idea 88

Organization: Children's Museum
Subject Area: Museums – Children
Keyword Search: children, culture, finances, education

Strategy

Redefine the concept of a children's museum in order to prepare for future growth, and incorporate an integrated marketing program for the organization to ensure profit and effective positioning well into the future.

Underlying Value

Values-driven, strategic marketing is best accomplished through a product development plan that includes creative services for customers. These initiatives will appeal to both the museum's potential corporate partners and a measurable market that is accessible through cost-effective networks.

Components

The Financial Literacy Initiative. The museum will announce to parents, educators and potential venture partners that it is ready to help prepare children for their financial future. Many adults acknowledge that they do not know enough about investments, how banking works or the process of creating a new business.

This integrated set of products, services and promotions would offer the museum several opportunities to generate sustainable income, attract co-ventures, and reach a broad spectrum of target markets, both national and international.

Execution

Allowance Kit. Both the museum and the corporate partner could market this interactive kit that teaches money management through stickers, games, puzzles and quizzes. The museum would not only help educate children and adults about practicing good money management skills, but would also benefit from product sales. The corporate partner would generate new business, promote a positive image and gain income from the kit sales.

Small Change. Working with a corporate banking partner, the museum would create a booklet about money management that is targeted to younger children. The booklet would help parents combat the "I want it" effects of television advertising. It would also teach holistic approaches to money–how to earn it, spend it, squander it, invest it and give it away. The banking partner could buy and distribute the copies, with a portion of the sales going back to the museum.

Idea 89

Organization: Children's Museum
Subject Area: Museums – Imagination
Keyword Search: children, imagination, creativity, play, greeting cards

Strategy

Redefine the concept of a children's museum in order to prepare for future growth, and incorporate an integrated marketing program for the organization to ensure profit and effective positioning well into the future.

Underlying Value

Values-driven, strategic marketing is best accomplished through a product development plan that includes creative services for customers. These initiatives will appeal to both the museum's potential corporate partners and a measurable market that is accessible through cost-effective networks.

Components

The Purposeful Play Initiative. Many families today are struggling to keep afloat financially while pursuing their own ambitions. Often, adults unintentionally communicate that there is not much room in life for fun. But, as psychologists and good parents know, play is not just the absence of work; it is an important part of every child's development. The museum is well positioned to serve as the champion of meaningful play by offering an integrated set of entertaining and educational products and programs for children, parents, educators and health care organizations.

Execution

Imagination Station. This interactive computer screen would allow children to paint pictures or write stories—certainly at the museum but also in the retail locations of corporate partners. One national greeting card company already uses computer-generated greeting cards. The museum computer could help a child write a song and would, for a dollar, print the music to be taken home for the family scrapbook or photo album.

The Imagination Station would serve as an on-site exhibit, a product with extensive sales potential and an exhibit-to-go. Imagination Station could also be rented by any number of retailers. They would attract families with children and keep the kids occupied with a creative and educational activity while a parent shops.

International Ambassadors of Play. This program would publicize the enterprise-oriented activities of the museum. It would involve children from all over the world, linked perhaps by the Internet, in a universal celebration of purposeful play. Kids would apply for the honor of serving their region, state or country as Play Ambassadors. In return, they would receive materials from the museum encouraging quality play and promoting its mix of products for sale. Companies that manufacture international foods would be likely venture partners, as would businesses that promote international friendship.

The State of Play Annual Report. This booklet would include a serious analysis of recent research into play and important things for parents to consider about play. It could also include discount coupons for children's activities and information like the following.

- Jokes and riddles

- Pages for coloring
- A listing of the best children's computer software, books, videos and music
- Recommendations for new toys and games.

The booklet could be presented by the museum's "Professor of Play" in a grand, boisterous ceremony that can be repeated in schools and community centers throughout the country.

Corporate partners, such as national restaurant chains and computer software companies, would help produce and distribute the State of Play Annual Report. The exciting and informative content of the report, as well as the coupons, would make this an appealing product for "kids of all ages" to purchase.

Idea 90

Organization: Museum Association
Subject Area: Museums – Management
Keyword Search: museum management, cultural enterprise, trade shows, museum store, mentoring, training, traveling exhibit, newspaper

---

Strategy

Become the primary resource for museums to learn how to operate more effectively, creatively and inclusively while offering valuable products and services to their current and potential customers. Operated by the association, this program, called the Cultural Enterprise Center, would be open to any association member. Its mission is to educate museums to think and act as entrepreneurial organizations.

Underlying Value

The need for the Cultural Enterprise Center is painfully apparent. Money has always been a critical issue for the vast majority of museums in this country. However, funding is often left to a discrete area of the museum. Fund raising often has an unpleasant taint to it; most museum administrators are far more comfortable with the world of scholarship than the worlds of business and finance.

The center will provide a new way of looking at how museums meet their mission. Additionally, it will:
- Invigorate museums to work toward self-sufficiency
- Assist museums in their moneymaking efforts
- Improve the quality of decision making on issues of enterprise among museums
- Define, promote and inspire best practice standards of enterprise that serve the public good
- Create added value membership in the association
- Become a profit center for the association.

Components

The center would be open to members only, with a potential for premium pricing for nonmembers, and would focus on three areas.

Training and Development. Through seminars and other training– from on-site assistance to a "graduate degree" in the core competencies– museums and other nonprofits would learn to become effective entrepreneurs. The center would also offer a step-by-step program to help museum executives discover their own unique skills as well as the resources that are available to achieve social enterprise.

Product Development and Marketing. This component would encourage and promote an array of joint ventures and products that museums could use to gain income. It would provide tools to museums that wish to work by themselves, with a network of other organizations, with corporate partners or through the association nationally.

Cultural Merchant Bank. This component would serve as a revolving research and development fund for museums that have good entrepreneurial ideas but lack the money to test them and make them a reality.

Execution

Training would begin with a guided enterprise self-assessment. Museum administrators would answer a series of questions about revenue-generation methods that interest them or currently present them with a challenge.

At the heart of the training, the center would offer a paradigm shift: museums and other nonprofits need to see themselves as businesses offering a valuable service to their customers rather than supplicants begging for attention.

Today's most innovative museum directors and other qualified cultural entrepreneurs would run the skills training. The center could offer speeches and presentations on topics such as conceiving product ideas, venture creation, partnership development, and incorporating excellence into its endeavors.

Ongoing seminars and workshops would be a cornerstone of the center. A typical seminar might focus on sales presentation–making the pitch to a potential partner. The greatest strength of this training format is the formal and informal exchange of information among participants.

Consulting and Mentoring. Museum administrators may understand venture formation but underestimate the impact of enterprise on organizational culture. They also must ensure that their enterprise choices remain appropriate for their unique mission and circumstances. With these concerns in mind, the center would offer consulting help to individual museums in a variety of forms. Services would range from a team of experts to a mentor who is available on an ongoing, as-needed basis. These individuals and technical assistance teams would provide earned income for the center.

Annual Enterprise Conference. This annual conference would celebrate and promote nonprofit and public enterprise. It could take place concurrently with or just before the association's annual meeting. The conference could also be presented in a videoconference format, linking enterprising museums across the country and allowing them to showcase their successes.

Graduate School for Social Enterprise. As part of the training, the center would offer a program in the core competencies nonprofit entrepreneurs need. Nationally known museum directors and others who are successful cultural entrepreneurs would teach the courses. They would be built on a case study format that encourages participants to work in small teams to apply the lessons to their situations. Local businesses and foundations that wish to help create financially astute and self-sufficient nonprofits and museums could pick up the cost. This investment in the museum will repay its initial cost, regardless of what organization foots the bill.

Product Development and Marketing. Membership in the center would provide instant access to the marketing and development opportunities described earlier.

Museum Gift Shop. Museum shops are traditionally a strong source of revenue, but they could be even stronger. The center would create a national network of museum gift shops that sell unique items developed by both small and large museums across the country. The center could also develop a national catalog of museum gifts that is easily customized to a particular museum. The catalog would target members and other likely customers. Fulfillment and billing would be accomplished jointly with proceeds routed back to individual museums.

National Newspaper. This option would be available to participating museums as a profitable replacement for a product that is typically a money-loser for most museums. The newspaper would blend local and national features with local and national advertising, creating the appearance of a publication that is generated by the local museum.

Joint Marketing Programs. This service could be available to graduates of the training program. It would offer museums of similar types across the country corporate co-ventures for similar exhibits. For example, a national railroad company could partner with a group of railroad museums to market books, videos and other products about the history of rail travel.

Travel. National partners could travel a circuit of graduate museums. The center could also offer graduate institutions an opportunity to be part of a nationwide "culture passport" that provides access to museums across the country. Companies could buy these passports for their employees or offer them as customer premiums.

Museum Trade Show. The center would host this show during an annual conference that allows museums to sell their best ideas to anyone who wants to buy. The center would invite corporate partners, retailers looking for new products to sell, ad agencies looking for new ideas for their clients, and other potential buyers.

The Cultural Merchant Bank. This bank would provide start-up money for cultural entrepreneurs. The association could fund programs similar to the existing Local Initiatives Support Corporation low-cost housing fund. LISC provides loans to developers who are willing to create low-cost housing, then funnels the repaid money into new projects. The association would be promoting exciting entrepreneurial efforts that could serve as fiscally responsible national models. In selected cases, the Cultural Merchant Bank would also take an equity position in joint ventures as its fee.

Poverty

Idea 91

Organization: Energy Aid Foundation for Low Income Families
Subject Area: Poverty – Energy Aid
Keyword Search: poverty, low income housing, energy, heat, energy conservation, electricity

Strategy
Increase awareness of and support for the foundation's efforts to keep citizens warm, encourage self-sufficiency, and educate citizens on energy conservation issues.

Underlying Value
The foundation is a valuable education and strategic marketing resource to the general public for a wide variety of businesses and corporations. It is in

a unique position to promote energy efficiency to help the environment and save individuals and companies money. The foundation can provide information to for-profits on how to equip and run their offices cost effectively, and it can help these companies gain recognition for their socially responsible practices. For both citizens and corporations, the foundation can link energy conservation with making a difference in the lives of low-income citizens facing a cold winter. The foundation could partner with participating utilities to give customers an incentive to conserve energy during peak consumption hours.

Components

The Enhanced Membership Initiative. This initiative would allow individuals to purchase a membership in "Energy Smart," a program that is managed by the foundation. It would be marketed primarily as a self-serving purchase opportunity because the range of benefits adds value to the membership. The program would be promoted through print advertising, inserts in utility bills, and promotional materials at home shows and energy-related retailers.

Membership would include a quarterly newsletter with articles on how to conserve energy, innovative energy technologies and conservation ideas for kids. The newsletter would also feature discount coupons for a variety of energy- and money-saving products and services.

Neighborhood Energy Watch. This neighborhood watch program would encourage neighbors to support one another in energy conservation. As a benefit of membership, citizens concerned about energy waste on a local level could access the tools and information they need to organize a watch.

The Energy Efficient Office Initiative. The foundation could create a set of materials for businesses that participate in the EEO initiative. Employees would have information on small ways to make a difference through posters describing how each action, whether turning off lights or recycling waste, affects the environment and energy efficiency. Businesses could buy the posters, and profits would go to the foundation.

A set of stickers for copy machines, computers and light switches could announce how energy conservation translates into dollars. More important, the stickers would translate employee efforts into help for a citizen who cannot afford her energy bill. For instance, it might say: "Turn this machine off every Friday night for a month and an elderly person will stay warm for a week." This would keep the employer's stewardship at the forefront of employees' minds.

The Peak Reduction Initiative. Customer billing and advertising would announce that savings realized by reduced peak period energy consumption will result in donations to energy assistance programs. The message sent to customers is: "During peak consumption hours, every dollar saved means twenty-five cents donated to keep a family warm in the winter."

This initiative creates income for foundation programs and links customer behavior with everyone's prosperity–public utility consumers, energy providers and low-income citizens.

Execution

Weatherization Promotion. This program would offer the "building community" an opportunity to be *about* building community. Any number of building supply companies could participate by pledging a percentage of profits from certain purchases to the foundation's programs for keeping citizens warm.

The company would communicate to customers that they are contributing to this initiative, either through billing inserts and promotional materials or during events such as a parade of homes or the "Ideal Energy Home Tour." Developers could participate each year by pledging a number of cents for each cubic foot of insulation they add to their new houses.

Glove Auction. This event would play on the dual meaning of a glove–both sporting mitt and clothing–to keep hands warm. The foundation would partner with a local or national baseball team to host an auction for a signed glove. Together, they would deliver the message: "When the team goes home for the winter, they don't need gloves." After the baseball season ends, auctions could be held during the lunch hour in high traffic areas of the city.

Meatless for the Heatless. This fund-raising event would feature an interesting twist. Invited guests pay for a dinner, but only bread and water are served. This indirectly communicates the poverty suffered by others. The money saved on catering would be donated to the foundation.

Idea 92

Organization: Low Income Housing Provider
Subject Area: Poverty – Housing
Keyword Search: low income housing, affordable housing, community programs, neighborhoods, poverty

Strategy

Become a valuable resource to business by establishing links between the organization's services and companies that have products and services to market. Develop clearly defined initiatives that communicate both the value of the organization's housing programs and the value of the corporation as a public purpose marketing partner.

Underlying Value

Since the organization specializes in a universal necessity (housing) it is well positioned to create a marketing strategy based on the appeal of linked prosperity. People like to purchase a product–something they need in their daily lives–that can help make a difference in the life of a needy person, or better yet, in the life of the entire community. Housing is one of the most visible links to one's community and to prosperity. This initiative builds on the organization's name or a descriptive trade name for organization-owned products.

Components

"Common Bonds" and "Common Threads" are descriptive trade names that symbolize the connection between average consumers and their low-income neighbors. Through these initiatives, the organization and its corporate partners would highlight the similarities and empathy shared by people regardless of their economic status or housing circumstances.

Execution

Common Bonds. This initiative could include anything from a certificate of deposit (CD) to a friendship kit for children that teaches communication skills and diversity appreciation. The organization's Common Bond brand would feature items that consumers can purchase to benefit programs in the organization's communities. It could also feature cottage industry products such as furniture or food products that are manufactured by the organization's residents.

Common Bonds could also provide a valuable way to create links with the real estate industry. It could become a product as well as a brand name and could be purchased by real estate agents. Instead of a plant or another housewarming or "thank you" gift, agents could pledge to purchase a Common Bond or charity check from the profits they earn representing a homebuyer or seller. The bond would go directly to the organization's programs. Funneling profits into low-income housing developments can be an effective cause-related marketing strategy for real estate companies looking to generate new business.

Common Threads. This initiative would feature the organization's brand of clothing and other sewn or woven products. Like Common Bonds, purchase of a Common Threads product would include a donation of profits to the organization's programs. One possible product is a Common Threads Security Blanket. This baby blanket would be knit by a resident and would come with a booklet on how to keep children safe.

Victim Support

Idea 93

Organization: Child Victim Advocacy Organization
Subject Area: Victim Support – Children
Keyword Search: child welfare services, parenting, human services, wisdom bank, resource for families

Strategy
Generate unrestricted income resources by packaging an existing reputation and expertise for the overall benefit of children, their parents and the private sector. Through relationships with corporations, this premier child advocacy organization will address an urgent need in the marketplace while developing systems that support and promote a high quality of life for children and their parents.

Underlying Value
The organization has a solid reputation for providing the "best of the best" information and networks for child welfare advocates and professionals. This initia-

tive can extend this reputation and the associated skills to a market segment of people who are able to afford access to systems, products and services that enhance the quality of life for their entire families. Widening this market impact will also increase the organization's ability to survive, grow and provide quality programs and services to its adopted populations.

Components

To encourage participation in these programs and establish a network of support from families and the general public, the organization would provide resources for families through the "Parenting Partners Network." The network will allow the organization to access new markets while providing services to its traditional market. The network will be based on the family's need to provide the best environment and resources for their children; the parent's need to play an active and confident role in the lives of his or her children; and the parent's need to share information and develop support systems with other parents.

Execution

Wisdom Bank. This 900 number telephone service comes with the option to receive a percentage of profits earned. The Wisdom Bank is a repository for parental wisdom on issues ranging from the how-to's of child rearing techniques to information on current parent resource services and ways to access them. It could also feature recent developments in child welfare reforms. The Wisdom Bank offers the organization an opportunity to disperse child welfare information through an existing data network and a mutual resource service for parents.

Business Write-Offs. This program encourages corporate and employee awareness about child welfare issues and collective participation in advocacy issues. The organization would form a coalition of participating businesses that already have national distribution. Businesses would donate a percentage of their business write-off totals for two weeks to one month of each year. Each company would, in effect, lower its business-related entertainment ceilings for the fundraising period. It would then donate to the organization the difference between the original ceiling and the actual amount spent during that period. The coalition would also issue a challenge to its members and employees. Corporations, corporate departments, and individuals would compete to spend the least amount during the organization's support period while still maintaining productivity. The organization would host this effective sales and client relations event annually.

National Points for People Program. Various nonprofit organizations throughout the country have initiated sports-affiliated pledge programs that match points gained with home runs, yards gained and quarterbacks sacked. One nonprofit organization in Denver has developed a program called Points for People. Donors pledge twenty-five cents to five dollars for each point gained through field goals by the Denver Broncos football team.

The organization could design and manage a similar initiative, a national Points for People, that uses achievements in national competitive events as pledge points. With the organization's affiliates as beneficiaries, the program would produce cost effective and sustained income. The organization's affiliates would sell and manage Points for People, establish income-producing partnerships with affiliates, promote the organization's interests through nationally recognized activities, and encourage the interest and participation of a market that may not normally be predisposed to donating to the organization. Specific pledge points could include:

- Medals earned by Olympic teams
- The Super Bowl
- The Major League (or Little League) World Series
- NCAA College Basketball Championship
- Corporate office pools that donate a percentage to the organization.

Idea 94

Organization: Service Provider for Crime Victims
Subject Area: Victim Support – Security
Keyword Search: support services, crime victims, security, road rage, children, vulnerable toys

Strategy

Create a support service that becomes a positive and proactive resource. In addition, secure a partnership that delivers measurable outcomes both in the "bottom line" and within the company's culture.

Underlying Value

The Brand. In the provider's targeted community, the "Provider X Support Service" programs would assist individuals who have survived experiences that are often tragic and terrifying, but its goal would not be exclusively responsive. The message it would communicate to citizens is: "We are here to help you learn how to maintain a safer lifestyle, rebuild circumstances and self-esteem for the future, and rejoice in the opportunity to thrive, not just survive." The corporate partner would benefit by initiating and strengthening its reputation as a strong shield against crime and victimization.

Components

Security in an Insecure World. As any police agency will attest, the main focus of crime reduction efforts should be on building awareness of ways to prevent crime in the first place. Citizens need to recognize how to avoid becoming victims in a wide variety of circumstances, and the key is information and training. This initiative would focus on educating citizens about how to avoid victimization. It could be built on a variety of possible products, services and promotions.

Execution

SecureFest. With consumers paying admission, this annual trade show would feature a variety of businesses and organizations that provide products and services related to security. Exhibitors would pay the service provider and its marketing partner for the privilege of participating. The corporate partner's products, services, and brands would be prominently featured. Products would include home and car alarm systems, computer virus protection software and personal products such as cell phones, beepers and flares.

SecureFest would also provide demonstrations and training sessions to educate the public on practical measures to improve personal safety. The trade show could move from location to location, building national awareness of the concept.

Answers to Road Rage. One of the most perplexing trends today is the phenomenon of angry and often violent behavior by motorists. A booklet of tips for drivers and their passengers could be pre-sold to auto repair businesses, parking lots, rental agencies and dealerships as a benefit to their customers. The booklet could also be featured with other information at SecureFest. Public seminars called "Reducing Road Rage" and "Responding to Road Rage" would also be offered both separately and at larger events.

Vulnerable Toys. This series would feature small toys, each accompanied by its own story involving a potentially insecure situation. The character would face a "vulnerable" (an insecure situation) about which a typical child would be concerned. The story would teach children how to keep this little friend safe. These products could also be marketed as collectibles. Sales could be carried out through retail outlets, direct mail and online orders, or distributed as a premium with the purchase of other corporate products.

The organization could use one of several models to develop this concept. Many American fast food chains have used plush toys, as well as coordinated books and games, to communicate environmental themes to children. Police departments regularly use soft animal toys to help reduce the trauma of victimization for children so they can discuss difficult situations.

Idea 95

Organization: Service Provider for Crime Victims
Subject Area: Victim Support – Safe Lifestyle
Keyword Search: crime, victim support, support line, self-esteem, confidence, kids, elderly, toys, security

Strategy
Create a support service that becomes a positive and proactive resource, and secure a partnership that delivers measurable outcomes both in the "bottom line" and within the company's culture.

Underlying Value
In the provider's targeted community, the "Provider X Support Service" programs would assist individuals who have survived experiences that are often tragic and terrifying, but its goal would not be exclusively responsive. The message this initiative would communicate to citizens is: "We are here to help you learn how to maintain a safer lifestyle, rebuild circumstances and self-esteem for the future, and rejoice in the opportunity to thrive, not just survive." The corporate partner would benefit by initiating and strengthening its reputation as a strong shield against crime and victimization.

Components
Confidence in the Future. One of the most important aspects of this support serv-

ice is that it addresses the emotional as well as practical consequences of crime. When a victim calls the support line or goes to the organization's Web site, the staff person who responds would ask questions not only about injury or loss of personal property, but also about the confusion and fear that result from such experiences. The support service representatives would be exceptionally well trained in helping victims regain their self-esteem and rebuilding their confidence.

And, there are practical reasons for this service. Citizens who continue to lack self-confidence, or who live in fear of going out or participating in their communities, make themselves and their neighborhoods less secure. Those who successfully recover from victimization look to the future with a positive outlook that is communicated to their families, co-workers and neighbors.

Execution

Confidence Kits. How does a person maintain a positive outlook about the future, especially after a frightening experience or loss of something valuable? The Confidence Kit could help with informative booklets and products for targeted groups. Corporations or brands would sponsor specific kits. These might include:

- Children – toys and games that promote rebuilding one's confidence
- Teens – tips that address smart dating and other social activities to maintain good self-esteem and personal safety. (These could be pre-sold to a sponsoring company, which then distributes them to incoming students of a university or other school.)
- Seniors – large print information, door locks and soothing music tapes
- Business owners – state-of-the-art software and technological devices designed to help businesses communicate a sense of confidence
- Tourists – products and tips on safe travel, and how to act or dress appropriately in different cultures.

These kits could be sold in a variety of retail locations, from do-it-yourself stores to toy stores and travel agencies.

National Toy Trade-In for Nonviolent Toys. Building on a program that already exists, the organization could partner with a toy manufacturer or toy store to combat the effect violent toys have on young children. A trade-in would invite children to bring their "violent toys" to the store and trade them in for a "nonviolent toy" and coupons for the sponsoring company's products. This event should be media-supported in order to garner extended visibility for the organization's mission as well as partnering companies' essential contributions. The Toy Trade-In is a great addition to the SecureFest concept (see Idea 94).

Rate Your Risk: A National Challenge. This annual program with national impact could feature the "Rate Your Risk Questionnaire." Citizens would fill it out so they can assess their vulnerability to various types of crime. It would appear in national newspapers and be available online or via mail if ordered through a toll-free telephone number. Even participating by completing the questionnaire would educate people about reducing the possibility of personal or property victimization. In addition, the campaign would help citizens by reporting each year on national progress toward a safer community and linking participants to resources that can further reduce their risk factors.

Idea 96

Organization: Service Provider for Crime Victims
Subject Area: Victim Support – Safe Communities
Keyword Search: city safety, support service, training, real estate, tenants, citizens against crime

Strategy

Create a support service that becomes a positive and proactive resource. In addition, secure a partnership that delivers measurable outcomes both in the "bottom line" and the company's culture.

Underlying Value

The Brand. In the provider's targeted community, "Provider X Support Service" programs would assist individuals who have survived experiences that are often tragic and terrifying, but its goal would not be exclusively responsive. The message it would communicate to citizens is: "We are here to help you learn how to maintain a safer lifestyle, rebuild circumstances and self-esteem for the future, and rejoice in the opportunity to thrive, not just survive."

Components

Celebrate a Safer City. The staff at this organization has a unique perspective on the impact of their services. They see that many of their clients become stronger, more confident and more assertive as a result of being assisted through the victim recovery process. And, they often note that victims of many types of crime often go forward in life with a positive, even celebratory attitude. These individuals are grateful for their survival; they have learned valuable lessons from their victim experience; and they have a more intense awareness of the goodness in life. Celebrate a Safer City would be a set of products, services and promotions that could convey the ultimate good available to individuals, families and businesses, along with a positive image not usually associated with victims.

Execution
Service Bureau for Real Estate Agents and Landlords. With crime on the rise, why not prevent unwanted crime by educating homeowners and renters. There is an open marketing niche for information that real estate agents and landlords can offer their customers. This provides them with a value-added service to help differentiate their services from the competition. The organization's expertise would go into creating booklets or videos that advise home buyers or lease seekers on how to live more self-assured lives by practicing effective safety measures at home. These products could also serve as effective recovery tools for families who have been victimized in the past.

Thousands of potential corporations, each hoping to deepen the value of their services, are currently seeking ways to help customers celebrate their new housing situation with practical resources. The service could also be purchased by one large company and distributed to its customers at no charge.

Turn Lights On and Turn Off Crime Campaign. One way for citizens to publicly acknowledge that they will act for a safer community would be to participate in a one-night, annual event sponsored by the organization and its marketing partner. Newspaper advertising could promote the campaign and, when paid for by manufacturers, discount coupons for light bulb purchases could be incorporated. Retailers would promote the event by posting in-store advertising, telling consumers that in honor of this campaign, when one package of light bulbs is purchased, the second package is discounted.

Citizens would be encouraged to leave their front entrance light on all evening, engaging in what experts believe is a simple action that is a strong deterrent to crime. The event could be organized locally, but promoted nationally.

Women

Idea 97

Organization: Social and Service-Oriented Women's Organization
Subject Area: Women – Stress Relief
Keyword Search: women's issues, stress, children, pampering

Strategy

Create an umbrella concept that can capture the public's imagination, provide an internal logic to a series of initiatives, and help position this women's organization as a regional pacesetter.

Underlying Value

Among the many issues facing women today, simply coping with the pressures of managing day-to-day life for themselves and their families is by far the most stressful. Recognizing that this stress touches almost every woman is the first step; providing coping skills is the second. This organization is equipped to provide the tools that help women face daily stresses, and become more focused, balanced and eventually, more successful in other areas of their lives.

Components

The organization would create a package of products such as books, kits, calendars and videos that can generate considerable earned income for the organization. These products, developed by the staff, would celebrate the achievements of women, offer the message of inspiration about people, and provide practical information that enables a busy woman to function more efficiently and therefore cope better with meeting her needs.

These products should be generic in concept, a customized package that is pre-sold at a wholesale price. The corporate customer would in turn use them as giveaways or premiums. They also have a retail value and could be sold throughout the country.

Execution

Mom's Mom. Since aging parents are a group that is demographically on the rise, there will be an increasing need for information and tools for caregivers. This booklet for adult children of aging parents could enable caregivers (usually women) to reduce the stress of their situations. A workbook format would be useful because the sections can be self-contained. The book should cover topics such as:

- How to know what is "normal" so you can look for signs of abnormal deterioration
- Handling the grandchildren's reaction to changes involving a grandparent
- Financial implications of aging
- Common psychological effects on families.

The organization could create many spin-off programs from this publication, including workshops, seminars and services such as financial and estate planning, legal planning and even counseling at the organization.

Pamper Me Discount Book. This coupon book could focus on providing discount service coupons that women want most. It would include a balance between fantasy or "wish list" services and practical ones. For services that currently exist, arrangements could be made with the provider to offer a discount. For those that do not exist, the organization might consider creating the service on a contracted basis. Some services that caregivers might want are:

- Personal wardrobe consultant
- Dry cleaners who deliver
- Grocery delivery
- Skin, nail or hair care
- Home plant care
- Facials and massages
- Car care
- Catered dinners at home.

Super Woman Juggling Kit. This product would be a spoof on juggling the four roles expected of today's women: mother, wife, home manager and professional. This four-piece juggling kit could instruct women on how to keep all the pieces "in the air." Instead of formless bean bags, this kit could feature pieces loosely shaped like a house, a baby, a husband and a briefcase. If the owner is a single parent, she only has to learn how to juggle three! This kit would offer a novel and unprecedented way to poke fun at a serious topic that affects a huge number of adults (more than sixty percent of the women in the United States alone).

Idea 98

Organization: Social and Service-Oriented Women's Organization
Subject Area: Women – Achievement
Keyword Search: women's issues, achievement, heroines, motherhood

Strategy

Create a marketing strategy that integrates successful sales, brand loyalty, direct customer communication, merchant support and an increasingly positive reputation as "the company that cares about women and the issues that concern them."

Underlying Value

Many issues cause women concern, but if the stated company wants to be known as the number one skin care company in the world, it must clearly articulate a marketing statement that accurately reflects its corporate character.

Achievement and recognition are two issues of great importance to most women. It is particularly important to women that their achievements be recognized and honored, since traditionally they have played a supportive rather than a leadership role.

Components

Four promotional themes would combine to form an effective marketing initiative that establishes the company's reputation as the leader in advancing the success of women.

- Twelve Who Care – achievements in caring
- Unsung Heroines – the achievements of "ordinary women"
- Mom's the Word – rewarding the contributions of mothers
- The First Time – marking life's achievements.

Execution

Twelve Who Care Award. The company could sponsor this award in recognition of outstanding achievements in caring by twelve professional women. At a highly publicized gala event, each recipient would receive a trophy in the shape of the company's logo, a certificate of recognition and a cash award.

The program could involve everyone. Customers would submit nominations on the Web site or through the mail, and the company would be able to collect and store certain marketing data for future use. Winners would be chosen by a blue ribbon panel comprised of business and civic leaders from all over the country. Artists would compete each year for the opportunity to design the official Twelve Who Care poster, which would become the focal point for all Twelve Who Care advertising.

Twelve Who Care Calendar. This calendar would feature one honoree each month with a photograph, biographical sketch and story in her own words about her achievement and what contributed to her success.

Unsung Heroines Magazine. Unlike the previous set of initiatives, this magazine would focus on the women who have exhibited extraordinary courage and resourcefulness in everyday life. The message of Unsung Heroines would be that ordinary women can achieve extraordinary things–that leadership can be exhibited in the common events of daily life. This magazine would feature an article about each one of twelve women, telling the stories of their accomplishments. The magazine would also run articles about Unsung Heroines in history whose affirmation with the chosen public purpose marketing partner touched the lives of others.

The magazine would be available for sale at store displays or through annual subscriptions by mail or Web site order. Subscribers would be entered into the marketing database and become eligible to receive advance notice of future promotions and special discount incentives. The magazine could highlight the nonprofit partner and have a special tear-out section with special discount coupons for company products.

Getaways for Moms. Motherhood is a demanding, nonstop job. The company could sponsor a Mom's the Word series of drawings for getaways ranging from Sunday brunch to a weekend holiday for two. Also, a monthly drawing would be held for a grand prize, such as a weekend vacation at a local Hilton, Forte or similar hotel. Most prizes, like meals, hotels, plays, concerts and even child care, would be donated by the various providers. In return, the provider would receive free advertising when prizes are announced on the Web site, on air or through other mediums. All prizes could bear the company's logo. In addition, the company might send each winner a kit filled with travel sizes of its products, along with a special Mom's the Word coupon book that entitles the mother to an additional ten percent off products. A special Mom's the Word booklet would provide hints on how to find personal time and make it enjoyable, when to call the doctor, quick and healthful recipes, and other topics of interest to busy mothers.

The First Time Club. The company would sponsor this club to celebrate the milestones of life that many women experience. Women can join the club by filling out a postage-paid membership application or by visiting the company's Web site and completing an online form. First Time Club members would receive a coupon book entitling them to periodic price reductions and a set of postage-paid notification cards. When the member marks a "First Time" event, she would complete a notification form and send it to the company. The company would add the information to its database and send the customer congratulations along with a free gift that is relevant to the milestone.

Idea 99

Organization: For-Profit Skin Care Company
Subject Area: Women – Achievement
Keyword Search: women, self-esteem, confidence, dreams, self-defense, technology, mentor, education, training

Strategy

Create a marketing strategy that integrates successful sales, brand loyalty, direct customer communication, merchant support and an increasingly positive reputation as "the company that cares about women and the issues that concern them."

Underlying Value

Many issues cause women concern, but if the stated company wants to be known as the number one skin care company in the world, it must clearly articulate a marketing statement that accurately reflects its corporate character.

Confidence and self-esteem are two issues of great importance to women. Some women may need help attaining the confidence necessary to achieve success and bolster their self-esteem. These initiatives can reinforce a perception among women that the company is the foremost sponsor of programs that help women realize their aspirations.

Components

Five themes describe effective marketing promotions that would establish the company's reputation as an organization that helps women realize their aspirations.

- Dream It, Do It – setting and attaining goals
- Step Up – mentoring program
- Pass it On – building self-esteem through public service
- Hear Me Roar – self-defense and protection
- CyberCare – women and the Internet.

Execution

Dream It, Do It: Setting and Attaining Goals. Most people have dreams, but making them come true takes planning. Knowing how to plan and set realistic goals is a valuable skill that can build self-confidence. This traveling exhibit that the company brings to communities in a van could feature workshops at churches, schools or civic centers and, in the case of small groups, in the van itself. An expert in goal setting techniques would accompany the van to its various locations. These interactive workshops would start with each woman receiving a workbook that contains a series of questionnaires. Participants would be invited to join in role-playing exercises. At intervals, women could purchase additional workbooks along with goal-setting books, video and audio products, and the Dream It, Do It Engagement Calendar.

Step-Up Mentoring and Internship Programs. A team of professional business associations from advertising, banking, retail, hospitality and other areas would arrange with their member companies to sponsor an annual two-week mentoring and internship program. Volunteer association members would agree to donate their time to work one on one with an intern, and their companies could agree to donate office space and supplies for the two-week period.

Any woman eighteen years of age or older would be eligible to win an internship. She could be a university student or a working woman. Step-Up application forms would be available at schools, universities, trade schools, libraries and retail displays. Applications would be mailed to the nonprofit partner's main office. Regional committees made up of professionals from the participating organizations as well as volunteers from the company would review the applications and choose interns.

Pass It on Points. This initiative would build confidence and self-esteem through service to others. Everyone has special talents and abilities that she can "pass on" to others. These women volunteers would receive points for each hour of service. Nonprofit organizations would punch or stamp point cards for each hour of volunteer service on a point card that resembles the frequent buyer cards offered by some retailers. Volunteers would redeem cards for products, and special bonus points could be given for every ten hours of service.

Hear Me Roar Traveling Seminars. A woman's self-esteem rises when she knows that she can protect herself when necessary. This initiative is about women speaking out and controlling their own destiny. Informal seminars could be held in shopping malls, parks, schools and libraries throughout the country. A self-defense expert or law enforcement official would give tips about self-defense and personal safety. The discussion could include tips on remaining safe when running errands, going to school or coming home late from work. Women would learn ways to secure their homes, cars and purses to avoid being victimized. They would also watch demonstrations of basic defensive moves that any woman can practice without training or special equipment.

CyberCare Show How. The Internet is here to stay, but this company knows it is a difficult tool for women to use if they feel intimidated. CyberCare would be the company's way of helping women build the skills they need to maneuver through cyberspace and take advantage of its benefits.

The central feature of the CyberCare program is the CyberCare Guide, which can take the form of a seminar or a book. Each guide would come with a workbook and card stock tip sheet, and perhaps coupons for discounts on Internet software and CyberCare mouse pads. The first phase of CyberCare would introduce the basics of the Internet, using the company's Web site in examples.

CyberCare videotapes could be sold to businesses and women's organizations as part of their in-house Internet training. The company might also coordinate a representative handing out product samples and coupons for discounts on CyberCare merchandise such as pens, note pads, mouse pads, drink cups, diskette holders, tote bags and T-shirts.

The company could also sponsor the CyberCare guide on its Web page. Women would be led through the guide step by step, and examples would look like the company's Web page. Along the way, women could choose options that give information about products and offer store coupons to print out and use for discounts on the company's products.

Idea 100

Organization: For-Profit Skin Care Company
Subject Area: Women – Health
Keyword Search: women's issues, beauty, aging, natural beauty, health, skin cancer

Strategy

Create a marketing strategy that integrates successful sales, brand loyalty, direct customer communication, merchant support and an increasingly positive reputation as "the company that cares about women and the issues that concern them."

Underlying Value
Many issues cause women concern, but if the stated company wants to be known as the number one skin care company in the world, it must clearly articulate a marketing statement that accurately reflects the company's corporate character. Vital and total beauty is one issue of great importance to many women. They look for products that contribute to their health and enhance their appearance. Since the skin care company has been producing these products all along, it is only natural that the company would employ a marketing strategy based on these assumptions.

Components
Four themes describe effective marketing promotions that would establish the company's reputation for helping women value their total being and not just one element of what society defines as beauty.
- Inside Out – the elements of vital beauty
- SOS (Save our Skin) – skin cancer awareness and prevention
- "Internatural" – good health and natural beauty
- Fine Wine – coming of age.

Execution
Inside Out Video Series. This series of five one-hour video recordings could come with a workbook. The videos would follow a television magazine show format with a number of segments about specific aspects of an issue (for example, an SOS segment might focus on planning for a "skin safe" vacation.) Each video would feature famous guests who talk about things they do to enhance that aspect of their own vital beauty. Exercises, in which viewers could participate either while viewing or afterwards, and complimentary workbook exercises would reinforce points made on the video. Skin care specialists from the company might host a portion of each tape and demonstrate ways that products contribute to all aspects of vital beauty.

Videos could be sold by subscription, phone, mail, a product catalog with other related items, and on the company Web site. Women could purchase one video or subscribe to the entire set for a special price. Videos would be sent to subscribers once a month. The company might also create an audio recording series.

SOS (Save our Skin) on the Street. With many people seeking suntans, skin cancer is becoming more prevalent. By partnering with a nonprofit cancer awareness program, the company could achieve the lofty goal of eradicating skin cancer. A program called SOS could become the company's signature event or initiative, enabling the company to become renowned as the skin cancer prevention company.

The SOS on the Street traveling van would stop throughout the country to present impromptu skin cancer awareness fairs at shopping centers, parks, libraries, health clubs and community centers. Outside the van, local dermatologists could join with the company's skin care expert to talk about skin cancer prevention and answer questions. A skin cancer video could play repeatedly so that people passing by could stop to watch and listen. A "children's corner" feature would help kids learn about putting on sunscreen, using tree shade for protection and wearing protective clothing. Company volunteers could pass out product samples and booklets that tell cartoon stories about sun protection.

Inside the van, doctors could conduct free basic skin cancer screenings. The company could sell sun-related products and demonstrate the correct way to apply them for maximum effectiveness. Companion items such as sun hats, visors, beach umbrellas and T-shirts would be offered for sale at a discount with the purchase of a sunscreen product. Another video could play inside showing attractive models in parks and on beaches wearing hats and applying sunscreen. The idea is to convince women that being smart is more beautiful than risking permanent skin damage.

International Mobile Health Fairs. When women purchase creams and lotions to help reduce wrinkle lines, they are admitting they want to look naturally beautiful with clear, glowing skin. But most women know natural beauty does not come from a jar. They know that good skin is about good health and proper skin care. International Mobile Health Fairs would travel around the country as a women's health clinic on wheels. Women would receive free cholesterol screening, skin cancer screening, blood pressure testing and glaucoma testing. A mobile mammogram could be stationed near the van. Outside the van, videos could air for the seated or passing viewer.

International Panel Discussions. Women's professional societies and other organizations are always looking for new programs to feature at meetings. The company's skin care experts could develop a panel discussion program. The panel would consist of the company's skin care expert and local experts such as a dermatologist, an exercise and fitness specialist and a general care doctor. The panel discussion program would be an ongoing event, traveling with the Mobile Health Fairs.

Fine Wine Online. As women mature, their perspectives change. Fine Wine is a "coming of age" program that helps mature women realize their health and beauty potential. With the personal computer boom, retired women are becoming a market to target through the company's Web site. The site would have a Fine Wine section that offers articles, vitality quizzes, interactive vitality exercises, games and an information trading post where women could trade information about subjects ranging from medical resources to hobbies.

Fine Wine might also offer periodic workshops on financial management, travel tips and health care. Women could register to win Fine Wine merchandise such as bath pillows, slippers, exercise equipment, pampering kits that feature the company's products and exfoliating sponges or shower mitts.

Idea 101

Organization: Women's Organization
Subject Area: Women – Networking
Keyword Search: women, networking, women's resource, directory

Strategy
Position the organization as the national resource of useful, practical, accessible information for women and by women.

Underlying Value
This women's resource organization is uniquely qualified to connect women with the people and information they need to solve problems and achieve success. The organization can create an umbrella strategy called "Information: Future" with the slogan, "If it's worth knowing, we have it." By providing very tangible, informative products, the organization cements its claim that it is what it promises to be. A key to success in this initiative is identifying needs, particularly of women between the ages of twenty-five and thirty-five.

Components

Women's Directory. The organization would create a magazine-like directory published annually for women. It could include a yellow page listing of services for women and a white page section with feature articles. Articles would offer city-specific information on health care, educational and career opportunities, neighborhood information, area recreation, shopping centers, how-to advice, critical emergency support services, fitness and nutrition. The directory would also feature an arts and entertainment section that includes theater seating charts. Listing in the yellow pages and advertising in the white pages would produce revenue.

The packaged style of the directory should be upbeat, lively, intelligent, up-to-date, and all sections should include interesting and well-researched resources, facts and features. Designed to look professional and functional, the directory would likely be used as a daily resource tool, found near a desk or phone. Many women would want copies for both home and office use.

The editorial or features section should explore broad interest topics such as:

- Career (helpful hints for the college-bound women, career tune-ups, relocation advice)
- Family (the infancy years, working families with children, empty nesting, returning nesters)
- The older woman (exercises for the older and wiser, stroke awareness information)
- Profiles of women leaders
- Health and nutrition
- Rights (changing your name, divorce and separation information).

Execution

Advertising. Local ads would be divided into white and yellow pages. White page listings would be open to businesses, organizations, services or products that would benefit area women. The yellow pages section should contain listings or services by area women and a comprehensive listing of local and national organizations serving women.

Distribution. Initially, the directory could be distributed in a fast-growing population center where the organization has a minimal impact. Distribution must be targeted to consumers based on the demographic and psychological profiles desired by advertisers. It should be distributed to women's events, organizations and seminars. It should also be professionally promoted and distributed to area bookstores, supermarkets and specialty stores. In addition, it could be mailed directly to government and corporate personnel, libraries and chambers of commerce.

Directories can also be pre-sold to corporations who can use them as a customer premium or giveaway. The directory should be of high enough quality to be sold in bookstores or used as a membership premium. Whenever possible, the organization should pursue wholesale options to avoid the time-consuming nature of individual fulfillment or retail sales.

National Network of Women's Directories. While the main model for the directory is established, the concept will be effectively "franchised" to other cities. Affiliates or partners could be solicited in select cities across the country to participate in a network of directories. The format, editorials and features would remain the same for all directories, but the local information would change with each city. The local partners would sell local ad pages to women in business, and all local ad revenue would remain in their hands. A secondary income source for participating affiliates might be directory selling rights after a controlled distribution number is reached. The organization would charge for the copies, and the affiliates would in turn sell them and split the revenue.

Index

catalogued by Idea number

A

"The Academy" Student Employment Service I-52
Accessible City Guidebooks I-84
achievement I-98
Adopt-a-Vineyard I-61
Adult Friendship Kits I-35
affordable housing I-32, 33, 36, 92
African American education I-16
African American Heroes I-16
African Folk Tale Video and Audio Series I-16
aging I-1, 2, 3, 4, 5, 97, 100
Allowance Kit I-69, 88
Angels in Action Award I-25
Animal Care Curriculum I-54
Animal Cookie Center I-20
Annual Enterprise Conference I-90
Annual Spring Sports Exchange I-38
Answers to Road Rage I-94
Aquatics Sales Kiosks I-39
aquatics university I-40
Architecture Rich Cities I-31
Auto Theft Prevention Kit I-26
automobile I-27, 67, 73, 74, 80

B

banking I-19, 60, 80, 88, 99
"Baseball" Cards I-27
"Be Prepared" First Aid Kit I-6
"Be Prepared" Road Safety Kit I-6
beauty I-55, 60, 100
Being There Handbook I-63
Bike Out of Crime I-26
Birthday Promotion I-38
Black American I-29

200 / Cold Cash for Warm Hearts

Black Map of the City I-29
blind I-83
Book Display and Sale I-20
Brag Book I-27
Brain Food I-58
Breeding Good Character I-53, 54
Bringing Help, Bringing Hope to Your Hometown I-44
Build-a-Home Board Game I-31
Builders Overstock Warehouse I-32
Bully-Proofing and other Good Ideas Booklets I-8
Business Membership I-36
Business Partners I-19
Business Write-Offs I-93
Buyers Home Inspection Booklet I-32

C
Cancer Relief Funding Covenant I-73
Cancer Relief Telephone Card I-75
care provider I-2, 3, 5, 7, 8, 9, 10, 16, 20, 76. 77. 81
Careers in Caring I-4
caring caravan I-44
Caring Coupons I-22
Caring Covenant I-5
Celebrate a Safer City I-96
Celebrating a Healthy America I-79
Celebrating Surviving Cancer Book I-76
Celebrating the Gifts of Life Initiative I-76
Celebrity Demonstrations I-20
Center for Creativity and Imagination I-50
Center for International Understanding I-48
Center for Youth Enterprise I-15, 52
character I-10, 12, 13, 14, 25, 33, 53. 54. 55. 59. 77
character development I-10, 12, 13, 14, 25
"*Check-In*" *Strategies* I-72
child development I-7, 15, 17, 18, 69, 85
Child Development and Care Centers I-7, 17, 18
Child Protection Program I-22
child welfare services I-93
Children's Book Competition I-50
Children's Challenge I-25
Children's Cookbook I-16
Children's Friendship Kits I-35
Children's World Fair I-47
Citizen Police Academy I-24
city safety I-96
Civic Certification I-37
Classy Compost I-54
Clothing Recycling I-13
Comfort and Joy Product Line I-2
Comfort Food Contest I-35
Comic Books I-16
Common Bonds I-92
Common Threads I-92
communication skills I-17, 69, 92
Community Barbecues I-35
community health I-78, 79, 80, 81
Community Mobilization I-44
community recreation center I-38
Community Service 900 Number I-46
Companion Card I-5
Company X Cork Recycling Program I-61
Company X Family Reunions I-71
Confidence in the Future I-95
Confidence Kits I-95
Conflict Management Software I-17
Conflict Resolution and Prevention Academy I-18
conservation I-13, 60, 61, 91
Cookbooks I-27, 35
cooking classes I-60
Cook-Look Books I-27

cork recycling I-61
Corporate Caring Edge I-5
Corporate Champion of Parent Teacher Associations I-12
Corporate Covenant I-73
Corporate Family Award I-68
Corporate Teen/Employer Training I-81
counseling I-17, 63, 64, 65, 66, 81, 97
Craft Carts I-87
Crafts Fair I-38
Create-a-Card Kiosks I-25
Credit Card Covenant I-73
crime prevention I-21, 22, 23, 24, 25, 26, 63, 68. 94
crime victims I-94, 95, 96
Crisis Intervention Centers I-64
crisis prevention I-63, 64, 65, 66, 67, 68
crops I-57, 58, 72
Cultural Enterprise Center I-90
Cultural Merchant Bank I-90
Cultural Sensitivity Software I-17
Customer Covenant I-73
Customer Involvement Initiative I-75
Customer Volunteer Days I-33
Customer-Engaging Products I-86
Cut-Out Books I-16
CyberCare Show How I-99

D
day care I-1, 7, 13, 16, 17, 18, 20, 54, 67, 68
Delivery Program I-7
Direct Services to Corporations I-7
directory I-101
disabilities I-77, 83, 84, 85
disaster relief I-44
Diverse Works Summit I-41
Docu-Dramas I-44
domestic violence I-13, 18, 65, 67
Donation Triggers I-71

Down to Earth Initiative I-91
Dream it, Do it–Setting and Attaining Goals I-99

E
Earn It! I-67
ecosystems I-56, 61
elder care I-1, 5, 37
Emergency Home Repair Corps I-44
Emergency Vehicles I-20, 44
emotional intelligence I-82
Employee Seminar Series I-65
employee volunteerism I-42
Employer Awareness Programs I-65
energy conservation I-91
Energy Efficient Office Initiative I-91
Enhanced Membership Initiative I-91
Enterprise Learning Opportunities I-34
environmental issues I-13, 47, 53, 54, 55, 61
Environmental Stress Audit I-65
EQ Profiles I-82
EQ Test I-82
EQ Training Workshops I-82
ethnic tolerance I-41
Executive Reproductions I-27
Executive Travel Health Fitness Kit I-38
Exercise Calendar I-38
extrapreneur I-34
Eye Product Purchases I-83

F
Face Painting I-20
Family Adventure I-6
Family Adventure Calendar I-6
Family and Friends Care I-81
Family Award I-68, 70
Family Computer Mini-Institute I-51

Family Conflict Indicator I-8
Family Coping Assessment I-17
family crisis I-63, 70
Family Health IQ Test I-78
Family Milestones I-6
Family Milestones and Memorabilia Kit I-8
Family Milestones Growth Chart I-6
Family Neighborhood Award I-68
Family Preparedness I-44, 78
Family Service Adventures I-70
Family Service Vacations I-33
family stress I-65, 67, 68
Family Time Capsule I-27
family tree I-63
Financial Competency, Conscience Management and Hands-on Learning I-19
financial education I-10, 19
Financial Literacy Initiative I-88
Fine Wine Online I-100
First Time Club I-98
Fitness Center I-20
Focus on Families Trust I-69
foster care I-8, 9, 10
free health clinic I-20
Frequent Purchaser Program I-77
friendly communities I-35, 36

G
garden path I-3
Get a Good Start with Your Pet I-54
Getaways for Moms I-98
Gifts of Gab I-41
Giraffe Project I-25
Glove Auction I-91
Good Start Affinity Programs I-54
Gotta Get Ready Booklets I-10
Gourmet Foods I-58
Graduate School for Social Enterprise I-90
Great American Lemonade Stand I-11, 52
Great Brand X Toy Challenge I-31

greeting cards I-17, 25, 35, 89
growth chart I-6, 8, 20, 33

H
Handicap Retrofit Service I-32
Handicapped Dolls I-20
Health Passport I-79
Hear Me Roar Traveling Seminars I-99
hearing impaired I-83, 85
Hearing Stimulation Kits I-85
Hearing Test or Screening and Podiatry Check I-20
Height/Weight/Temperature I-20
Help for Do-It-Yourselfers I-32
Helping Families Balance Work and Home I-72
Heritage Hamlets I-27
Heroines I-98
Hidden Treasures I-87
Historic Neighborhood Award I-28
Historic Trails Project I-55
home improvement I-32, 37, 57
Hometown Action Network Initiative I-80
horse I-53, 54, 55
housing I-5, 31, 32, 33, 34, 35, 36, 45, 63, 90, 91, 92, 96
How Kids See Violence I-18

I
"I Wish I Didn't Have To" Chores I-32
ID the Blind Person I-83
Imagination Station I-89
Important Role of Schools I-70
In Honor of Community Service I-43
Individual Membership I-23, 36
infant hearing test I-85
Information Area I-20
Inside Out Video Series I-100
"Insight" Private Label Brand I-83
International Ambassadors of Play I-89

Index / 203

International Business Enterprise Forum I-15
International Costumes I-47
International Etiquette I-47
International Institute I-48
International School Curriculum I-15
International Audio Library I-15
International Teleconference on Youth Choices I-47
Internatural Mobile Health Fairs I-100
Internet Pen Pals I-9
Intervention Center Franchises I-64
Inventions Competition I-49
investing in others I-77

J
job fair I-4, 23
Jogger's Map I-38
Joint Marketing Programs I-90

K
Kids on Kids I-67
Kids on the Go I-14
Kids on the World Wide Web I-14
Kids Ports I-15
kiosks I-8, 27, 39, 49
Kits for the Do-It-Yourselfers I-32

L
Learning Passport I-14
lemonade stand I-11, 52
Lifelong Learning with the Station I-37
Literacy Mentors I-10
Living Well Covenant I-80
Living Well: A Health Care Service to Businesses and Their Employees I-80
Living Well: A Service to Corporations and Their Employees I-79
low income housing I-32, 45, 71, 91

M
Make a Difference Day I-70
Managing My Money Clubs I-10
MASH Units I-44
Meatless for the Heatless I-91
Membership in the "Rescuers League" I-59
Membership Programs I-66
mental health I-81, 82
mentor I-10, 37, 90, 99
Mini-stores I-6, 27
Mom's Mom I-97
Moms and Tots I-51
Mom's the Word I-98
Museum Gift Shop I-90
museum management I-90
Museum Passport I-86
museum store I-90
Museum Test Drive I-87
Museum Trade Show I-90
Mysteries of the Region I-87

N
National Fundraising Telethon I-21
National Newspaper I-90, 95
National Points for People Program I-93
National Service Summit I-70
National Teleconference I-21
National Toy Trade-In for Non-Violent Toys I-95
Neighborhood Energy Watch I-91
Neighborhood Service Pack I-24
Neighborhood Watch I-21, 24, 37, 68, 91
NJC: Not Just Cans I-13
No More Victims Kit I-22
No Place Like Home I-5
Nutrition Center I-82

O
Old Pro Handyman Services I-44
Old Pro Resource Center I-45

organically grown produce I-59
Organization Private Label I-58
Organization Tree Swing I-60
"Organization" Smart Card I-34
outdoor adventure I-6, 55

P
Pamper Me Discount Book I-97
Paper Models of Famous
   Buildings I-31
Parent Sabbaticals I-8
parent support network I-69
Parent/Family Exchanges I-48
parenting I-6, 7, 8, 9, 15, 20, 22, 51,
   63, 64, 65, 66, 67, 68, 69, 70, 72, 93
Parenting Center I-20, 51
Parenting Desk I-69
Parenting Kiosks I-8
Parenting Power Digital
   Dialogues I-8
Parents Information Center I-20
parent-teacher association I-12
Park Police Partners I-53
Pass It on Points I-99
Passport to Education I-23
Patents for the Poor I-56
Peace Dolls I-47
Peace Fantasy Camps I-47
Peace Prize I-47
Peak Reduction Initiative I-91
Peanut Butter Paint I-62
pen pals I-9
Pence Parade I-77
pet I-8, 53, 54, 76
phone I-10, 17, 20, 21, 37, 42, 71, 72,
   75, 84, 93, 94, 95
Playspaces I-7
Plush Toys I-60, 94
police academy I-24
Pop-up Book Series I-31
Portrait I-20
Postcard Book I-27
poverty I-22, 33, 56, 57, 58, 91

Pre-sell Strategy I-81
Preservation Products I-55
Preservation Wagon Train I-28
Preserving the Best of our Past I-55
private school I-11, 15, 49, 50, 51, 52
Product Reward Pricing I-41
Products for Children I-37
Profiting from the Earth Financial
   Mechanisms I-60
Public School Solicitation I-29
Purposeful Play Initiative I-89

Q
Quality Character Cards I-53
Quality of Life Partnerships I-31

R
radio station I-20, 37
Rate Your Risk: A National
   Challenge I-95
real estate I-96
(Really) Small Business Award I-34
recycling I-13, 14, 61, 91
Regional/National Day I-30
Remember Me Theme I-76
Rent-a-Gramps Program I-1
Responsible Pet Ownership Program
   I-54
Rewards of Healthy Living Initiative:
   Incentives for Success I-79
road rage I-94
road safety kit I-6
Roses for Moms I-81

S
Sacred Sites Tiles I-30
Safe for Seniors I-63
Safeguard Initiative I-74
Safety Comes First I-78
Safety Snoop Kit I-26
Savings Bonuses I-19
Savings Plans I-5
Scholar in Residence Program I-15

Scholarship Contest I-12
School Bonds I-12
scout I-6, 26, 37
Screening Saves Lives I-78
Secure-Fest I-94, 95
Security Blankets I-35
Security in an Insecure World I-94
security systems I-74
seeds I-57, 59, 62, 78
Seeds of Promise I-57
self-defense I-99
self-esteem I-8, 16, 18, 22, 24, 65, 67, 94, 95, 96, 99
Senior Companions Comforter I-2
senior housing I-5, 63
Sensory Olympics I-83
Service Bureau for Real Estate Agents and Landlords I-96
Service Credits I-4
Service Currency I-37
Service with Your Pet Program I-54
Sharing the Pride I-87
Sibling Celebration I-69
skin cancer I-78, 100
Small Business Administration I-15
Small Change I-82
Small Comforts I-2
Smart Families Safety Kit I-6
Snack Shop Strategy I-12
Solutions WarmLine I-17
Soothing Sunday I-2
SOS on the Street I-99
State of Play Annual Report I-89
Steps to Safety I-18
Step-Up Mentoring Programs I-99
Sticker Sets I-16
Street Law Kiosks I-49
stress management I-81
Student/Class Exchange I-48
stuffed animal clinics I-20
Summer Opportunity Fair I-23
Super Women I-97
support line I-95

T
Tantalizing Scents I-60
Teacher Exchanges I-48
teen employment I-67
Teen Gift Registries I-9
teens I-8, 9, 10, 18, 23, 63, 64, 67, 68, 81, 95
telethon I-21
Tips from "Your Academy" I-51
TNT Consulting Service I-9
Toy Trade I-13, 95
trade shows I-10, 90
Travel Pillow I-2, 70
Travel Security Systems I-74
traveling exhibit I-19, 21, 29, 90, 99
Treat Seats I-14, 69
tree swing I-60
Trustworthy Handyman of the Middle Class I-32
Turn Lights On and Turn Off Crime Campaign I-96
Twelve Who Care Award I-98

U
Unsung Heroines Magazine I-98
Unused Sick Days I-5

V
Values Growth Chart I-33
Values with Value I-12, 13, 14
Vendor Cooperation I-6
victim support I-93, 94, 95, 96
Village Street Scenes I-27
vineyards I-61
Virtue in Action I-77
visually impaired I-83
vulnerable toys I-94

W
water sports I-39, 40
Weatherization Promotion I-91
Welcome to the Neighborhood I-29
Where Does Peanut Butter Come

From? I-62
wine I-61
Winners Wall I-76
wisdom bank I-93
Women's Directory I-101
women I-97, 98, 99, 100
women's resource I-101
Wooden Toy Van I-84
working families I-7, 42, 62, 68, 72, 101
World Record for Volunteering I-42
Wrist Phones I-72

youth awards programs I-25
Youth Bank I-19
Youth Card I-19
youth development I-6, 7, 8, 9, 10, 14, 15, 16, 17, 18
youth enterprise I-10, 15, 19, 52
Youth Enterprise Fairs I-10
Youth Insurance Policy I-23
Youth Social Enterprise Recognition I-34
Youth Trust I-19

Y

yellow pages I-52, 101
Yes I (Eye) Can: Celebrating Abilities and Eliminating Stereotypes I-83

About the Authors

Dr. Richard Steckel is the president and founder of AddVenture Network based in Denver, Colorado (USA). He has earned an international reputation as a consultant and speaker on nonprofit social enterprise and for-profit strategic corporate citizenship. For more than twenty years, he has helped organizations the world over to develop earned income strategies, products and services. From his company's offices in Melbourne (Australia), Auckland (New Zealand), Vancouver, British Columbia (Canada), and Surrey (England), he has helped over two hundred organizations.

Before his current work, he was Executive Director of the Denver Children's Museum, where he introduced innovative ideas that made the museum a national model of the earned income approach to fundraising.

Dr. Steckel is the co-author of the best-selling book *Filthy Rich: How to Turn Your Nonprofit Fantasies into Cold, Hard Cash* (revised and updated 2001), *Making Money while Making A Difference: How to Profit with a Nonprofit Partner* (High Tide Press, 1999) and *In Search of America's Best Nonprofits* (1997).

A book under development is *Milestones* (by Dr. Steckel and his wife Michelle), an essay with photographs on tolerance and common human experiences.

Dr. Steckel serves as a volunteer on the boards of the National Security Archives, Corporate Philanthropy Report, and NESsT (the Nonprofit and Self-sustainability Team). He was a director of E Source Corporation, a subsidiary of the Rocky Mountain Institute. He is also an Associate with Sustainable Cities Trust in New Zealand.

In addition to his work as a consultant, writer and volunteer, Dr. Steckel has taught on the faculty of the University of Auckland (NZ) and the University of Massachusetts at Amherst (USA). His work in Amherst included the development of an online independent study course on strategic alliances.

Dr. Steckel has also served as a director of international programs for a Boston-based technical assistance organization, a community organizer on New York's Lower East Side, and a producer of public service media on social issues. He holds a doctorate from Boston University, a master's degree in social work (community organization) from Adelphi University, and a bachelor's degree in history from the City University of New York. He advises the Consultative Group on International Research and its marketing organization, Future Harvest. He works with member affiliates in Kenya, Cote d'Ivoire, the Philippines, Mexico, Columbia, Peru, Sri Lanka, Malaysia, and the Hague.

Elizabeth Ford is a classic survivor of the late 1990's technology and Internet boom who has since shifted her focus to the nonprofit sector. Her background includes public relations work with MCI, a successful IPO with an Internet marketing company in Boston and serving as the primary marketing manager of a "software-turned-Internet" company in Denver. Currently, she manages all development activities for a behavioral health care organization in Denver and is pursuing a master's degree in business administration.

Traci Sanders has worked as a writer, researcher and editor for over twelve years. Her projects have ranged from children's fiction to international business to marketing strategies for nonprofits. She lives in Colorado with her husband and two children.

Casey Hilliard holds a master of arts degree in anthropology and is currently an instructor at Metropolitan State College in Denver. She worked as Dr. Steckel's assistant from 2001 to 2003.